OXFORD AND THE IDEA OF COMMONWEALTH

Sir Edgar Williams
CB; CBE; DSO; Deputy Lieutenant
Warden of Rhodes House, Oxford, 1951–80

Oxford and the Idea of Commonwealth

Essays presented to Sir Edgar Williams

edited by Frederick Madden and D.K. Fieldhouse

CROOM HELM
London & Canberra

© 1982 Frederick Madden and David Fieldhouse
Croom Helm Ltd, 2–10 St John's Road, London SW11
British Library Cataloguing in Publication Data

Oxford and the idea of commonwealth.
   1. Williams, *Sir* Edgar
   2. Commonwealth of Nations – Historiography –
Addresses, essays, lectures
   3. Historians – Oxfordshire – Oxford – Addresses,
essays, lectures
   I. Madden, Frederick   II. Fieldhouse, David
   III. Williams, *Sir* Edgar
   907'.2'09171241   DA16

ISBN 0-7099-1021-5

Printed and bound in Great Britain by
Biddles Ltd, Guildford and King's Lynn

CONTENTS

EDITORS' PREFACE

Three years ago, to fill a sudden gap in the programme of the Oxford Commonwealth seminar, Ronald Robinson asked Freddie Madden, as the old man of the Oxford tribe who had lived through some part of the story and had known many of the actors, to give a paper on the historians who had held the Beit Chair. When, in 1980, Sir Edgar (Bill) Williams was retiring from the Wardenship of Rhodes House, it was decided to mark the occasion by devoting the Trinity Term to a series of papers which would pick up and expand themes, opened up by that paper, on the role of Oxford and its members in the history and historiography of the Commonwealth. Those papers, polished, slightly abridged, but still in their informality reflecting the fact that they were read after tea to a group who knew each other and their foibles well, constitute the main body of the text. Unfortunately we were unable to include a chapter by Kenneth Robinson on Commonwealth studies elsewhere than in Oxford — a summary of his forthcoming detailed report on the interest in that subject in British universities during the first half of the twentieth century. It was not then clear that these papers would ever be published; but subsequently both the Rhodes Trustees and the Administrators of the Beit Fund provided generous financial support for publication and we express our gratitude to them. We would also like to thank Dr Gowher Rizvi, Rhodes Scholar (Trinity and Balliol) for his quiet, discreet, and efficient help in organizing the seminars and preparing the book for publication; and Hilary Walford, whose experience in publishing has imposed whatever stylistic uniformity this diversity of scripts possesses.

This is a *Festschrift* for Bill Williams — soldier, administrator, biographer, and imperial historian; but, unlike many of its kind, it has a central coherence because all the contributors were attempting to answer a single question from different standpoints: recognizing the work being done by others in other universities elsewhere in Britain and overseas, what particular contribution did Oxford make to the forging of the idea of Commonwealth and to the writing and teaching of Commonwealth history?

Frederick Madden and David Fieldhouse, 1981

INTRODUCTION: SIR EDGAR WILLIAMS

Greig Barr

'Bill' Williams was one of the young Oxford historians of the 1930s whose academic career was interrupted by the Second World War. A Postmaster of Merton College and later a Harmsworth Senior Scholar, he had been elected to a Junior Research Fellowship of the College in 1937 after a short absence when he was an assistant lecturer of the University of Liverpool.

The summer of 1939 found him already in uniform as an officer of the 1st King's Dragoon Guards. In his case the army was no drab task-master. His service in North Africa, Italy, and north-west Europe was distinguished indeed. Recognition of his exceptional skill in disentangling the complexities of military intelligence brought rapid promotion and he served under that demanding master, General Montgomery, as GSO1 of the Eighth Army and as Brigadier General Staff I of 21st Army Group.

Formal connection with Oxford was re-established in 1945 by his election to a fellowship of Balliol College of whose Governing Body he remained a member until his retirement in 1980. After six years (which included service in 1946 and 1947 with the United Nations Security Council Secretariat) he was appointed Warden of Rhodes House. Henceforth for Oxonians generally, not only for Rhodes Scholars, he was 'the Warden'.

His Wardenship (to which office the Secretaryship to the Rhodes Trustees was added in 1959 for the first time) was notably successful in keeping fresh the ideals of the Rhodes Trust during twenty-nine years of change in and outside Oxford. He provided efficient and respected, if not always easy, solutions to the many problems arising from the Trust's world-wide 'constituencies', from the affairs of the Scholars, and from the management of Rhodes House itself. 'Things were always "done right" at Rhodes House,' a former Scholar has recorded. At least equally important were the Warden's sympathy, hospitality, and tact. Not all Scholars are at once at home in Oxford and their backgrounds differ widely. In Warden Williams they found wise advice, all the better for being candid, and a friend whose wit delighted. They naturally took to him their worries, sometimes their miseries, academic, social, or emotional; and affection was increased

1

not lessened if silliness or pretension were so described.

Not only the Rhodes Trustees but the university as a whole succeeded in making use of his talent and of his experience. He did not pretend to find university administration an unworthy chore and he served in more ways and for more years than perhaps anyone else of his generation. He was a member of Hebdomadal Council from 1951 to 1980; he was a Curator of the Chest and its Vice-Chairman, one of the Curators of the Parks and their Chairman, and a Pro-Vice-Chancellor. His style was distinctive. Unlike some academics with a taste for responsibility, he never talked over much, but his incisive, often humorous contributions when they came frequently ended debate. He had sensitive antennae for the ridiculous and for the log-roller. The former could entertain but the latter lived in peril. As a chairman, his apparently light rein, the entertaining *obiter dicta*, went with an exceptional speed in business. The unimportant was made manifestly so and only those who thought that a respectable meeting should last a long time were dismayed. In his appreciative essay on James Stephen, Permanent Under-Secretary of the Colonial Office and 'Mr Mothercountry', he comments that the power to delegate was a mark of a good administrator. That capacity Bill Williams certainly showed.

The service was not to the central bodies of the university alone nor to Oxford alone. He was a Fellow of Queen Elizabeth House, the Chairman of the Nuffield Provincial Hospitals Trust, a Radcliffe Trustee, and a member of the Oxford Regional Hospital Board. He was Chairman of the Administrators of the Beit Fund. Somehow he found time, maybe not unwillingly, to be Treasurer and later President of the University Cricket Club. Further afield he was a member of the Devlin Commission for Nyasaland in 1959 and, twenty-one years later, a Commonwealth Observer of the Southern Rhodesian elections. He was also concerned in the 1960s in the establishment of new universities and chaired the Academic Planning Committee for the University of Warwick.

These later responsibilities no doubt gave pleasure to one whose first scholarly interests had centred upon imperial history. Pre-war research was concerned with the earliest years of the colony of New Zealand. With the outbreak of the Second World War the projected book did not appear, though articles were published on the Treaty of Waitangi and on the Colonial Office under James Stephen. So too was an article on 'The Cabinet in the Eighteenth Century'. (Readers in the Bodleian Library have noted for many years that this article has been so frequently consulted since 1938 that its now grubby pages are barely legible.) On his return to Oxford, he joined Professor Harlow's Commonwealth history seminar and came to be recognized as especially knowledgeable on a wide range of subjects in nineteenth-century colonial history – sometimes, indeed, to the irritation of the Chairman. He was much in demand as an examiner, not least in the new B.Phil. in Commonwealth and American History; as a judge of (for instance) the Beit and Herbert Prizes; and as an adviser and encourager of many researchers and potential researchers, not only among Rhodes Scholars. For ten years in the 1960s he was Chairman of the Committee for Commonwealth Studies.

A major debt owed to him by scholars and indeed by browsers was his editorship of the *Dictionary of National Biography* from 1949 until 1980 and his own contributions, for instance the entry on Sir Winston Churchill. One may suspect that this was an agreeable responsibility, for he could certainly communicate the pleasure he found in the odder aspects of the characters of those described and of those who described them.

Why are his services so often sought and so greatly appreciated? He has a quick instinct for the right answer and takes unabrasive trouble to convince others. Certainly not cold, he is a delightful companion, amusing with a fund of excellent stories, sympathetic. Liking others, others like him and they trust him.

Part One

OXFORD ORIGINS

Part One

OXFORD ORIGINS

1 THE COMMONWEALTH, COMMONWEALTH HISTORY, AND OXFORD, 1905-1971

Frederick Madden

In 1905 the first Beit Professor of Colonial History, Hugh Egerton, was appointed. But of course Oxford men had been making and writing imperial history long before that date. Indeed, the first propagandist for overseas empire, Richard Hakluyt, came from Christ Church and among his contemporaries were Walter Ralegh of Magdalen and Humphrey Gilbert of Oriel. Later William Penn was at Christ Church, and Christopher Codrington, Governor of the Leewards, had been a Fellow at All Souls. Oxford prime ministers had naturally had to deal with colonial problems – George Grenville of the Stamp Act, Shelburne, Portland, Liverpool, Canning, Gladstone, Peel, Salisbury, Rosebery – to name but some of the Housemen. And a whole wall in Christ Church Senior Common Room is inhabited by Indian Governors-General – Wellesley, Minto, Amherst, Bentinck, Auckland, 'Clemency Canning', the eighth Earl of Elgin, Northbrook, and Dufferin, with the addition of Irwin (Halifax) in the twentieth century: Curzon and his two predecessors – Lansdowne and the ninth Elgin – were at Jowett's Balliol (Curzon and later Chelmsford were also Fellows of All Souls).

In the 1760s, on the eve of American secession, William Blackstone, Professor of Jurisprudence and an MP, had, in lecturing on sovereignty,[1] rehearsed the omnicompetence of parliament which some Americans felt impelled to challenge successfully; and Horace Walpole, of King's Cambridge, witnessed to the strongly anti-American opinion in both Oxford and Cambridge throughout the events leading to the loss of the American empire. John Wesley, who had left Lincoln College to make a small contribution to the Great Awakening in America, denounced the American pretensions as strongly as any high churchman. In the 1840s Herman Merivale, Drummond Professor of Political Economy, had given lectures on *Colonization and Colonies*[2] and then gone to 14 Downing Street as permanent under-secretary to the Colonial Office (when James Stephen in reverse had retired thence to a Cambridge chair) to make policy: Merivale afterwards went on to the same position in the India Office. Elgin had left Christ Church for a fellowship at Merton and then to a governorship first in Jamaica and then in Canada

7

to implement the Report of his father-in-law, Lord Durham. J.R. Godley had gone from 'The House' to found a Christchurch in New Zealand. And Goldwin Smith of University College in the 1860s, even as Regius Professor, before he left for exile in Cornell and Toronto, had in no way moderated his lifelong dislike for empire as a source of expense and weakness to Britain.

But what of the academic interest in empire before 1905? There had been a few questions of imperial interest in examination papers for the Final School of Modern History – very occasionally on American independence, even less often on Canadian self-government, once on the Great Trek. But there were quite a number of questions (not annually, but fairly regularly) on India – on Clive, Hastings, and, in 1905, on the Mutiny. Indian studies – especially in languages, where in 1886 a separate Honour School was established – were already long entrenched in the university: indeed, in the 1680s the East India Company had – at John Fell's persuasion[3] – founded four annual scholarships at Oxford. Two hundred years later Christ Church founded a mission in Calcutta. By 1905, then, Oxford had been teaching Indian Civil Service (ICS) probationers for a quarter of a century, and the Indian Institute, open since 1884, housed teaching rooms and a large library. Concern for the ICS had been fostered by Jowett, the Master of Balliol: in the 1880s Balliol had half the Indians and half the ICS men in Oxford with Arnold Toynbee as their special tutor. Readerships in Indian law and Indian history had been established in 1878: S.J. Owen, the first Reader in Indian History held the post for the next thirty-five years. There was already a remarkable Sanskrit collection in the Bodleian Library: it was soon to be the largest outside India. And there were in Oxford, too, other links with overseas empire which had nothing to do with the ICS or government: the Ashmolean, for example, had Pocahontas' father's cloak, and the Pitt Rivers collection, brought to Oxford in 1883, had provided a wealth of anthropological and archaeological material, in part from the colonies.

Nevertheless there were no special imperial papers: imperial history was not a separate discipline; it was part of British history and imperial questions were set in outline British papers. They were not blandly uncritical: it was safe enough now historically to question George III on America, or to find clay feet on a heroic Clive. History was history in those days: no scholar thought it proper to write history of events within the last half century. (Only after the Second World War was the fifty-year rule modified to a mere thirty years for the Public Records.) Current affairs could be left to journalists and other writers of fiction.

But the past could have a message and historians a mission. Macaulay (a Cambridge man) could in the mid-nineteenth century glorify the Revolution of 1688 to justify mid-Victorian liberalism; and Seeley (another Cambridge man) in the 1880s, believing that 'history was past politics and politics present history', could in his *Expansion of England* (1883) advocate a Greater Britain of the future resting not on an Indian empire but on British settlement colonies overseas. The *fin de siècle* was marked by an undermining of Victorian self-confidence: the Pax Britannica was severely challenged by rivals, competitors, and internal critics. Assurance became faltering and, by reaction in some, strident. A frantic concern for security lead some to think of imperial self-sufficiency once more; a new mercantilism; a new imperial association, even federal perhaps. Though those on the lunatic fringe which campaigned for such a cause were very few indeed, on that fringe as usual academics were much in evidence. Three successive Directors of the London School of Economics (Reeves, Hewins, and Mackinder, who had founded the School of Geography at Oxford) preached this woolly federal cause: so did G.W. Prothero, the collector of Tudor documents, from Cambridge and Edinburgh. On the other hand it was Sir Frederick Pollock, Corpus Professor of Jurisprudence at Oxford, whose own research and special committee reported such federation to be totally impossible. The Boer War pricked the bubble of expectations. Already opinion, with an almost Calvinistic sense of guilt, was returning strongly to a more sober dedication to imperial responsibility.

It was on the eve of the Liberal landslide and the Campbell-Bannerman government (including from Jowett's Balliol Asquith and Grey, but not Milner) that the Chair of Colonial History, endowed by Rhodes's colleague, Alfred Beit, from his diamond and gold profits in South Africa, was established at All Souls. Yet within three years the new Beit Professor was questioning whether Oxford was worthy of an imperial role. It was perhaps apt — if you accept Max Beloff's 'imperial sunset'[4] — that it was only when the empire was receding into the past that a history chair was created to study it. But it was for that generation, in want of assurance and oblivious of Beloff's precipient doom, not merely a recognition of the need to develop the field of colonial history, but an opportunity to recall with some confidence the past and to search that past for lessons for an imperial future. And Oxford, traditionally a cosmopolitan university, had now become a Mecca for colonial scholars: by Rhodes's own will in 1902 Rhodes Scholarships had been instituted and the first Rhodes Scholars, including

W.M. Macmillan from South Africa and Chester Martin from Canada, were in Oxford preparing to sit Finals. Chester Martin was the first winner of the Beit Prize established at the same time. He won it in 1908 with an essay on the set subject — Lord Charles Somerset's governorship at the Cape. Others who won the prize before Egerton resigned in 1919 included Lewis Namier and A.L. Burt (Burt was also awarded the Herbert Prize that year — 1913) who wrote on Closer Union; Harold Laski in 1914 on the third Earl Grey (he went later that year to teach at McGill); and Murray Wrong, in 1915, already a Fellow of Magdalen, with an essay on the American Loyalists. Wrong was to succeed Coupland as Beit Lecturer in 1919. Apart from Curtis, the other lecturers who served with Egerton were W.L. Grant and James Munro, who both edited collections of the Acts of the Privy Council in their tenures; Grant later in Queen's (Kingston) was concerned too with the recruitment from the Dominion of men for the British Colonial Service.

The interest in imperial studies at the turn of the century was not of course exclusively an Oxonian phenomenon. It had long been the concern of the Royal Colonial Institute to promote education in colonial history and geography at school, university, and extra-mural levels. The Cambridge local lecture syndicate had been persuaded to run six courses on the empire and from 1893 a university extension course in imperial history. At London University in 1912 Sidney Low had unsuccessfully advocated a School of Imperial Studies, but a standing committee on imperial affairs was established instead.

Hugh Egerton was elected to the Oxford Chair in 1905 — to the little enthusiasm of Milner, one of the electors — and gave his inaugural the following April: six years later Lionel Curtis from New College and Milner's Kindergarten was appointed to one of the two Beit Lectureships provided for at the same time, but he was rarely in Oxford, preferring to perigrinate around the empire forming Round Table groups. (The other lectureship was never filled, though in the 1970s the Beit Administrators found a little money temporarily to appoint an additional Junior Lecturer, Robert Holland, then Gowher Rizvi.) Egerton took a First in Greats at Corpus; studied law as a barrister; served as private secretary to an MP — cousin, Edward Standhope, who fatefully went to the Colonial Office in Salisbury's Cabinet; fell under Seeley's influence, became secretary to the Emigrants Information Office in 1886; produced a reference book on the colonies and then published in 1897 his *Short History of British Colonial Policy*: a pioneer textbook. He contributed to two volumes of the *Cambridge Modern History* (1902), edited Molesworth's speeches (1903), revised Sir Charles Lucas's *Historical Geography of the British Colonies* (1888 and 1904), wrote two booklets for the League of Empire on *Colonization* and on *Empire Builders* (1906), and published a life of *Raffles* (1897). As professor his lectures (now deposited in typescript in Rhodes House) covered the subject, didactically and perhaps a little dully, from seventeenth-century America to twentieth-century Dominions. With W.L. Grant, the first Beit Lecturer, he collected some Canadian constitutional documents (1907); published (under Curtis's influence) the texts of *Federations and Unions in the British Empire* (1910) embracing the New England Confederation of 1643, the Albany plan, and the constitutions of Canada, Australia, and South Africa — a book immediately prescribed for History Finals; produced an outline history of British foreign policy (1917), and after retirement a book on the *Causes and Character of the American Revolution* (1923), and the *Dictionary of National Biography* article on Joseph Chamberlain.

Better as tutor than lecturer, he acquired a profound knowledge which enabled him as chronicler to show the wide range of the subject, and as cartographer to view its frontiers and to establish its general features. His approach was that of a pioneer: we owe to him the first spadework. He did not mistake vision for history: most of the entries for the annual Royal Colonial Institute essay competition, established in 1883, he could dismiss in 1913 as 'of little merit': in the university section one at least was inferior to any of the school entries and another merely 'a vision in heroic couplets'. In his own work, though there was a massing of fact, there was no subtle or sensitive mind analysing, questioning, or seeking new sources. But clearly he believed that imperial history did not stop and there was continuity from afar to the present. This concept of continuity became the peculiar stamp of imperial history at Oxford.

Reginald Coupland, the Beit Lecturer till 1918, succeeded Egerton as Professor in 1920. It was not perhaps an obvious election, for when he had replaced Curtis in the lectureship in 1913 he had little more than an amateur's interest in colonial history. Indeed his First was in Greats and his fellowship at Trinity in ancient history: but he had fallen in with Curtis who had persuaded him of his duty to learn about modern, not ancient, empires. Together they had been concerned earlier in 1913 (with Milner, J.G. Lockhart, James Allen, and others) in the foundation of the Ralegh Club, a forum of empire and colonials, whose arcane ritual and toast 'The Empire of the Bretaignes' survived into the second half of the twentieth century (though Ralegh's prayer, from which that phrase and its reference to 'the attendant daughter islands about her' was taken, refers presumably to Ireland, Man, Scilly, Wight, and the Channel Islands – not perhaps the most impressive of empires). Moreover the Round Table movement, founded with support from the Rhodes Trust in 1909 by Milner and Curtis, had a strong Oxford base, and during the First World War Coupland, who published as a morale-booster the war speeches of Pitt, acted briefly for the first of several occasions as editor of the quarterly by the same name. When Egerton resigned, the risk of appointing a non-specialist was taken: the electors to the Chair sought to give stature to the new discipline of imperial history by setting a fine Greats mind to the field; a first-class scholar was better than a third-rate expert: if only universities continued to believe so.

Coupland set about learning his new subject with vigour. Character-istically he began with a life of Wilberforce (1923); a decade later this interest in evangelical humanitarianism led to a short popular account of the *Anti-Slavery Movement* (1933) and, via *Kirk on the Zambesi* (1928), to his notably original work on *East Africa and its Invaders* (1938) and *The Exploitation of East Africa* (1939), followed by *Livingstone's Last Journey* (1945). It was a tribute to his prescience as well as his wisdom in that period of complacent imperial optimism that two-thirds of his inaugural lecture in 1921 should have been devoted to grasping the nettle of Commonwealth race relations. In the mid-1920s came his own sketch of *Raffles* (1926) – obviously now the feudal service (or required peppercorn rent) for the Beit Chair – which to his delight (when I told him) found its way on to the detective shelves in W.H. Smith's (his library overflowed with detective stories); a distinguished, fresh, and sensitive *Quebec Act* (1925) wherein naturally he found the Commonwealth long adumbrated by British toleration in 1774 for alien people and custom; and a similarly broad-based and sympathetic account of the *American Revolution and the British Empire* (1930) which looked beyond the schism of 1783 to an English-speaking alliance and 'special relationship' in the twentieth century.

This teleological optimism, discreet not exuberant, also infused his interpretative lectures given in 1935, *The Empire in These Days*, and even his edition of the Durham Report ten years later. He was led by way of French Canada to an understanding of other nationalisms: for example, in his posthumous study of it in Wales and Scotland (1954), but much earlier and increasingly in contemporary India, which came to absorb him. He had always shown a keen interest in current affairs: Coupland's enthusiasm, and the regard felt for him in government circles at home and overseas, drew to the prestigious Ralegh Club on Sundays a galaxy of distinguished speakers and thereby the liveliest and most influential undergraduates of the 1920s and 1930s to share a confidential ringside view of events.[5] Through Amery and Curtis he had been instrumental in bringing Smuts to the Sheldonian to give his Rhodes Memorial Lectures in 1928, which were ultimately to prompt Lord Hailey's African *Surveys* (1938-45); and C.R. Fay came to give a Beit special lecture on the imperial economy, 1600-1932. But Coupland's visit to India in 1923 on the (Lee) Royal Commission on the Superior Civil Service kindled a special concern and a generous sympathy for the subcontinent and its problems (he was also an influential member of the (Peel) Royal Commission on Palestine in 1936 for which he drafted the report). He wrote a pamphlet for Harlow's Ministry of Information propaganda series, *Britain and India* (1941); an account of the Cripps Mission (1942) to which he had been attached; three reports on India for Nuffield College (1942-4) of which (as of PPE in Oxford) he had been a founding father; and the gist of those recommendations, together with a deft historical background for the general reader, *India, a Re-statement* (1945).

It was in this context that Coupland was most magisterial, walking with ministers and princes and Congress leaders. A patrician, tall, slight, dignified, he wrote with felicity and grace in a neat fine hand; he lectured gently and quietly with persuasive charm. He supervised with a long rein[6] but was readily available if needed. His lectures (like those of Harlow later) were for the Colonial Service men – the surveys wide-sweeping, compelling, quietly amusing. In his elegant writing there is deceptively much thought and weight, but for the most part (as was the fashion) he used only printed sources. Where Egerton had established the chronology, Coupland was opening up the subject, seeking (intuitively sometimes, sensitively always) to dig more deeply, to understand, and to interpret. His pupils were encouraged, and expected later, to break into the Colonial Office papers, missionary archives, and private collections. His personal relations with them and with colonial cadets, Rhodes Scholars, Indians, and the few Africans around were easy and friendly: the more bitterly did he feel Eric Williams's personal attack on him in *Capitalism and Slavery* (1944). By the time he retired – prematurely and somewhat wearily – in 1949, he had seen imperial history grow to become one of the most popular special subjects in Finals, and in constitutional documents almost half the finalists were doing some Commonwealth history.

Among those who had taught the subject were of course his successors as Beit Lecturers: among them Murray Wrong, a Canadian Fellow of Magdalen, who made a collection of detective stories and edited Charles Buller on Responsible Government (his widow married the second Warden of Nuffield); Kenneth Bell of All Souls and Balliol, who had taught briefly at Toronto University, and on retirement was ordained as vicar near Coventry, and who wrote on Shakespeare, compiled a number of source books, and (later with John Maud) organized the Tropical Administration Course; W.P. Morrell, who did a block-busting thesis on the colonial policies of the 1840s which in its range and detail puts to shame the narrow limits of years (even months) and country (even provinces) of our latter day D.Phils, and also contributed to the *Cambridge History of the British Empire*; Vincent Harlow, who also held in plurality the first and only Keepership of Rhodes House Library; and Kenneth Wheare, who had in 1933 won the Beit Prize with an essay on the set title – inevitably – 'the Statute of Westminster' (W.L. Burn won the Herbert Prize that year). There were also other imperial historians and tutors. Sir Charles Lucas, who, on retirement from the Dominions department of the Colonial Office, was writing and editing many volumes on the empire (and comparing it with the Roman empire) at All Souls; Keith Hancock at All Souls in the mid-1920s (there to his own surprise and briefly a Round Tabler) and again after the Second World War as Chichele Professor of Economic History, giving a new economic dimension to the subject before going to help found the Australian National University; Sir Vincent Lovett, Reader in Indian History, who (it is said) bored generations of ICS probationers; Edward Thompson at Oriel who alarmed them; and the young men newly-graduated – Richard Pares, Colin Dillwyn,[7] Eric Smith, and Bill Williams. Perhaps closest to Coupland of them all, in approach, in Nuffield, and in concern for the present, was Margery Perham, with a whole continent almost to herself.

Though Coupland inspired colleagues and friends with deep affection, few shared his particular Commonwealth idealism (he was of course no Curtis federalist and became estranged from him) or commitment to current affairs. Most kept their heads down in Bodley, the Codrington, and the Public Record Office and their ears open to the many tutorial essays. Since 1928 the colonial history special subject based on a collection of documents made by Bell and Morrell (on Morrell's thesis) and with some help from Wrong, had won between 12 and 15 per cent of the undergraduate market. And after 1945 PPE, too, had its own

Commonwealth special subject, resting on Kenneth Wheare's main interest — the Statute of Westminster and federal government (the latter subject urged on him as Gladstone Professor by Lord Beveridge) and serviced by three *quondam* Beit Scholars (himself, Kenneth Robinson, and myself). Coupland died in November 1952, on the gangway embarking for the Cape and a revisit of all friends and old haunts (including *Isandhlawana* (1948), the subject of his penultimate book). He had deposited with his publisher that morning the manuscript of the first of a projected series on nationalism in the Commonwealth. By then Harlow had been Beit Professor for two years.

It is convenient to pause at this point to consider what had happened during the first half century of the Beit Chair. As we have seen, imperial history had established itself as a popular subject. It was, however, a gain in numbers rather than in academic prestige: it was considered an easy option securing few Firsts; indeed, many of those going on to the new research degrees in imperial history had taken other options in Finals. There were now many more (other than the increased number of Rhodes Scholars) from Commonwealth countries, coming to do both first degrees and research. Research tended to be about British policy towards a particular colony in a given period, and the periods were much longer than they are nowadays. It was a question largely of working carefully and intelligently through the Colonial Office files — the in-and-out correspondence — of telling an attractive narrative, and of making sensible comment and conclusions. The emphasis was predominantly metropolitan but it was already beginning to change to one of interaction between British and local influences and institutions.

Rhodes House in many ways changed the environment for imperial history. Open since 1929, it provided lecture and seminar rooms and a library — the only dependent library in Bodley with a subject catalogue. There were indeed plans to have buildings round the lawn, to separate the American and Commonwealth Reading Rooms, and to have bedroom-studies for visiting academics; but these did not materialize. Herbert Baker, the architect, kept a vigilant eye even on the wattage of the light bulbs and the only building done since 1929 was the enormous lower basement. But some of Baker's symbolism has endured: the first time many of us encountered the name Zimbabwe was on the staircase up to the library. Until the post-Second World War pressures there were no central desks or tables in the Reading Room, only in the named alcoves. The clientele was relatively small, more intimate and friendly than it became after 1945: researchers kept desks piled with their books for years. There were also the Colonial Service cadets — the Tropical Africa Administration Course from 1926, then the Devonshire Courses. In 1938 there was a special summer conference on colonial administration at Lady Margaret Hall. In the early 1930s Harlow was in the study in Rhodes House. He and Pares ran the weekly Commonwealth history seminar, working the 1830–60 period so hard and in such intense detail that it was almost killed off by the late 1930s. After the war the Beit Lecturer inhabited the Hawksley room and taught never less than twenty-five hours a week during the next ten years. Coupland lectured there, only on a general outline course, with the cadets in mind. The Ralegh Club, the Overseas League, the Victoria League, Missionary Societies held meetings there. So did the Majlis — an 'India in Oxford', founded in 1908 — often torn by inner dissension, as many including S. Bandaranaika of Christ Church (1919–23) witnessed. After the war, in 1946, with no Keeper or historian in the study, it was decided to have as invigilator in the Reading Room an assistant librarian who actually knew what was within the covers of a book so that he could give advice on bibliographies for weekly essays. (I was that librarian before being elected a year later to the Beit Lectureship.) Returned veterans demanded teaching and wanted individual tutorials: it was an enormous teaching load, given the popularity of the colonial options. Rhodes House was bursting at its seams not least in the hard fuel-crisis winter of 1947-8 when it filled with hundreds seeking first warmth and then coffee.

There were other centres for imperial studies too — Nuffield College and the Institute for Colonial Studies. Nuffield provided a more flexible and modern base than All Souls for Coupland's concern with India and perhaps more particularly for Margery Perham. In 1941 the University's Higher Studies Fund made a large grant to Nuffield for colonial research. From this Martin Wight's book on the Legislative Council spawned a series on colonial legislatures, and a team interested in Nigeria — 'a tropical dependency' — (Mars, Forde, and Bower) pioneered the study of development economics which achieved status when Unilever established a chair for Herbert Frankel, a pupil (like Lucy Sutherland) of W.M. Macmillan's. There had been from 1926 a committee dealing with the Tropical African Administrative Course, later the Committee for Colonial Studies. When research was stimulated, books, reports, and newspapers were collected, and research workers gathered, an Institute was established with rooms on the ground floor of Margery Perham's house in Bardwell Road, then in South Parks and Keble Roads. She was Director while she held the new Readership in Colonial Administration.

Then, after a period when the Directorship was in commission, Sir
Reader Bullard and Sally Chilver were successively Directors. By the
time I was appointed, the Institute occupied part of Queen Elizabeth
House in its own right — with a sort of Dual Monarchy, which worked
very amicably; but, as was planned before I took over in 1961 when
Bill Williams was Chairman of the Committee for Commonwealth
Studies, the posts of Director and Warden were merged when Lewis
Wilcher retired.

But to return to the Coupland era. Among the fashionable seedbeds
in Oxford between the wars were the Sunday teas: Gilbert Murray had
his liberal philanthropist League-of-Nations set on Boar's Hill, Chevasse
had his evangelicals in New Inn Hall Street, etc. There were also groups
interested in Commonwealth. Coupland was at home in All Souls rather
than on Boar's Hill (he was unmarried),[8] but there was John Buchan
at Elsfield Manor with open house for an invasion of those known in
the family as the 'Amalekites'. Buchan, whose Newdigate prize poem
in 1897 had been on the Pilgrim Fathers, commuted daily third-class
to London for Nelsons or the Commons, and devoted weekends to
Elsfield, including reading the second lesson (I sometimes read the
first): T.E. Lawrence, John Strachey, Frank Pakenham, Leslie Rowse,
Arnold Smith (the first Commonwealth Secretary General), and two
Beit Prize men, Gladwyn Jebb and Alan Lennox Boyd, were among
those who dropped in for tea. At Elsfield Manor it was serious rather
than clever conversation which won respect. And there were also groups
critical of empire: the Coles, much influenced by Marx by way of the
inaccuracies of that liberal propagandist from Lincoln College — J.A.
Hobson — with G.D.H. Cole, who detested liberals (he was Reader in
Economics at University College before becoming Professor of Social
and Political Theory at All Souls and Nuffield) leading the new Fabians
firmly away from the Webbs' infatuation with Joseph Chamberlain;
Auden and Betjeman were there, so were Hugh Gaitskell and Kenneth
Robinson; but, when Margaret Cole insisted on living in London, G.D.H.
held these gatherings at lunch-times and midweek, not Sundays. But
India almost alone constituted their interest in empire. Two other
nuclei of anti-empire in the years immediately after 1945 might be
mentioned here: Tommy Hodgkin, later to be the first Lecturer in the
Government of New States (Africa) in the mid-1960s (the Asian lecturer
was Sir Penderel Moon of the ICS and the Quit India movement), had
been briefly in the Colonial Administrative Service in Palestine, but
as Secretary to the Extra-Mural Delegacy (Rewley House) in 1945-52

did a great deal to organize adult education in Ghana, Nigeria, and Uganda; and Leonard Barnes, for four years in the Colonial Office, then in South Africa for twice as long, then Director of Social Training (Barnett House), whose *Duty of Empire* in 1935 had critically examined the purposes and results of imperial rule with a clear commitment to the positive obligation of trusteeship.

The last years of Coupland's tenure saw an increase in the number of posts in colonial studies. Using Colonial Development and Welfare funds, the university established lectureships in history, agriculture, and economics, primarily to teach for the Devonshire Courses. George Metcalfe, the last of Coupland's research assistants, and then George Bennett were the historians; Geoffrey Masefield taught agriculture and Hla Myint economics. After a time these posts were taken over fully by the General Board and became normal university lectureships. There was also a new lectureship in colonial administration, briefly held by H.A.C. Dobbs, then by Francis Carnell. This became the Lectureship in the Politics of New States.

Vincent Harlow, the last of the Beit Professors to give an inaugural lecture, did so in November 1950: it lasted an embarrassing hour and twenty minutes. As an undergraduate he had read essays to Egerton, but had been supervised for his thesis on the seventeenth-century Caribbean by the Regius Professor, Sir Charles Firth. He returned from four years in Southampton to Rhodes House Library in 1928 and to the Beit Lectureship in 1930. In his shirt sleeves and with a handcart he had physically involved himself with the transfer of Bodleian books to Rhodes House (just as Hugh Allen had helped move the School of Music from the Clarendon to Holywell). Harlow had drafted the classification and subject catalogues. In 1938 he was elected to the Rhodes Chair at London when A.P. Newton, a physicist turned colonial historian, retired. Harlow was a shy man, outwardly austere and even intimidating, but with a genial, even gentle, humour, especially when with children. One often-repeated story of his concerned the hilarious occasion when, coming into the dark after a seminar in Balliol, he involved me in breaking into and trying to drive away a car identical to his own which was parked immediately behind his in Broad Street.[9]

Though still in his later years (like Coupland) a pro-consul *manqué*, he was, despite experience on a commission to British Guiana, much less the public man and much more the devoted scholar. His early work had concerned Barbados, Christopher Codrington, and seventeenth-century colonizers and exploration, especially Ralegh. He contributed to two volumes of the *Cambridge History of the British Empire*, notably with a fine piece on the New Imperial System for volume II; he failed to produce a long-promised chapter for volume III and I had to do it — amid normal teaching — in four months to fulfil his deadline. He edited the Imperial Studies series, the Pioneer Histories, and Longman's pamphlets on the Commonwealth. As the Second World War grew closer he wrote the concluding chapter to Alan Bullock's book on *Germany's Colonial Demands* (1939). But before then, though he continued to live in Old Marston, his London chair and flat enabled him to work long in the Public Record Office and the British Museum and to write many chapters on *The Founding of the Second British Empire, 1763-93*, the most substantial piece of scholarship to appear from Oxford imperial historians in the century. (Hancock's *Survey* perhaps runs it closest, though Hancock's forte is more in interpretation and less in detailed research.) During the war Harlow worked for the Ministry of Information in the Empire Information Service and was drawn from Elizabethans and Stuarts to twentieth-century Commonwealth. He had to cope with suspicions among the professional administrators in the Colonial Office and spent much time on a Board of Education project for a school history of the empire. After the war — a six years' gap — he was dissatisfied with his pre-war chapters and it is evidence of his devoted scholarship that he decided to reorganize and to rewrite the complete book; so volume I did not appear till 1952.

By then he had returned to Oxford to the Beit Chair, now at Balliol. He refounded the Commonwealth history seminar on Fridays, sometimes in Balliol, sometimes in the Beit Room in Rhodes House: it was *his* seminar. Bill Williams and I were required to attend, but did not appear in the credits on the lecture list until some years later. It had a large and distinguished clientele of future Commonwealth historians from Britain, Canada, Australia, New Zealand, South Africa, the West Indies, and Africa; many still came then from Commonwealth universities to Oxford to get doctorates.[10] Harlow rarely came into Oxford more than once a week: to lecture to the Devonshire Courses,[11] to return his pupils' chapters, and to hold the seminar; the rest of the week he laboured at his book, his Royal Commonwealth Society contacts, and Old Marston Church.

Harlow's lectures were attractively fluent, incisive, and wide-ranging: they were infused with a staunchly Christian interpretation and a deep sense of legacy, and seminars were more than a little serious and morally earnest. Above all he believed strongly in the wholeness of imperial history. Indian and African history should make a contribution to the whole. Colonial history as a specialism was not enough; it must be integrated with an understanding of metropolitan history: indeed, from Egerton's time and before, the only way to attract an undergraduate clientele was to 'sell' imperial history as an extension of British history. In his inaugural he emphasized that

> insularity distorts — but that distortion is not rectified by inserting large slabs of 'British empire' history (as such) into curricula already overburdened. What I have tried to say . . . is briefly this. It is required of the historian and rightly required that he should see, and present, men and their thinking *whole*. Accordingly he must correlate the social, the economic and the political, which deepening specialisation tends to keep in separate compartments. To do this with comprehension he must be explicit in testing the whole range of facts against the enduring values of the civilisation which informs them.

He rejected the idea that history was just historical research: it must mean *understanding*, not controversy. Historians must search for new evidence but 'documents must not take the scholar into an ivory tower'.

If mere colonial history was unnecessarily narrow, he sought other dimensions. So he urged pupils from the Colonial Office files into the Treasury, the Admiralty, the Board of Trade, and the Foreign Office. He gave emphasis to administrative, commercial, and economic history. He found his own Whitehall experience in the war (as did those two distinguished scholars of eighteenth-century empire, Richard Pares[12] and Lucy Sutherland, at the Board of Trade) immensely useful in the study of empire. He saw imperial history as a study of people and communities: the effect of Britain on peoples outside Britain and of peoples overseas on Britain. What horrified him (despite his wartime propaganda as *Veritas*) was instant journalism or pathological judgement based on sense of guilt or injured race-pride, where the object of such *soi-disant* history is not objective analysis, but the use of the past to vindicate present claims. It was a perfectionist ideal, to which we ought all still to aspire; but week after week it could be schoolmasterly and suffocating. Analyse, question, formulate — it was an exacting discipline, and many Commonwealth historians benefited. But analysis was impaired without synthesis, he would add — with a characteristic wide sweep of his arm. The duty of any historian was to seek by all means and avenues to *understand* and to understand against the contemporary, not the modern, background. That was Harlow's message.

Then one Friday evening in December 1961 David Fieldhouse, George Bennett, and I waited in the Beit Room for him to take the chair at the seminar, and he did not come. (David Fieldhouse had succeeded me as Beit Lecturer three years before when I had moved into the Readership occupied first by Margery Perham and then Kenneth Robinson.) Vincent Harlow had died suddenly in his car in Gloucester Green. By April 1962 I had completed volume II of *The Founding of the Second British Empire, 1763–93* on which he had been working that afternoon. Longmans redated my preface as May 1963 and published the book at the beginning of 1964. Such is the devotion of publishers to historical accuracy.

By then, after another interregnum — my second caretakership — we had Jack Gallagher as Beit Professor.[13] The Commonwealth seminar was now at Nuffield, and the Friday morning teaching seminars on sources were already in progress. Gallagher arrived in April 1963 and brought an exhilarating 'wind of change' to Oxford imperial history, which had become too inbred, too dedicated, too seriously minded in its concern with the goal of a Commonwealth, present and future. He renewed and invigorated the subject. He had vitality, dash, sometimes a stimulating irrelevance, and often a new irreverence. In a preface to a book an old pupil refers back to Falstaff in his tribute to 'sweet Jack, kind Jack, true Jack, mad Jack'. Gallagher could be an iconoclast. His mind delighted in juxtaposition of contrasts. He had wit, a devastating turn of phrase, a rich sense of amusement. His frame of historical reference was not just imperial, but global. Though he might exaggerate to stimulate debate, he would never over-colour an untruth into a truth, or vice versa; nor would he dismiss another's conviction, but rather approach it with an alternative explanation. His talk was so fertile in ideas that we groped around among his cast-offs, seizing them, weighting them, and claiming them maybe as our own.

Indeed we were close — a team for the first time — cross-stimulating and cross-fertilizing. Commonwealth history became fun: no longer largely a Commonwealth promotional industry, but part of the world of scholarly entertainment. Harlow had been embarrassed by flippancy, finding (for example) an anonymous article on 'Cwthmanship' in the Christmas number of *The Economist* (1958) almost profane. Unlike Coupland or Harlow, Gallagher was no Governor-General *manqué*, rather a licensed jester, veiling sanity with laughter. Commonwealth history was now emphatically no longer only metropolitan: Gallagher looked at the ground roots on the perimeter. In 1937 Richard Pares, in a distinguished article on 'The Economic Factors in the History of Empire' had asserted emphatically that 'the most important thing in the history of an empire is the history of its mother country'. In part this was a declaration of interdependence, a denial that imperial history was an exclusive, autochthonous discipline, inwardlooking, and self-sufficient. Forty years later, though the truth of Pares's assertion remains still undeniable, the emphasis had quite rightly shifted to embrace a detailed understanding of *local* societies and terrain: to see empire not so much as moving outward, as coming in, from Britain and affecting an indigenous or expatriate people. Jack Gallagher could hold both these concepts in balance: he held the wholeness of the Commonwealth experience intact. On the History Board he firmly withstood the proliferation of regional special papers. To his chagrin a regional balkanization did begin to take place in the late 1960s. The Indian seminar, successively under C.C. Davies, S. Gopal, and K. Ballhatchet, had, indeed, always been aloof and exclusive, save in a brief period when Davies was yoked with Lucy Sutherland; but Gallagher's own interest of course embraced South Asia. But by the late 1960s African history seminars increasingly drew off its specialists into their own coven. The whole might seem only to reconvene when Indian or African topics were specifically on the Commonwealth history paper; and the Commonwealth history seminar was not the only loser by these absences.

The same phenomenon had, of course, already struck history seminars elsewhere. The flood of overseas Canadians, Australians, New Zealanders, and South Africans was drying up, as they did their doctorates (often more appropriately and closer to their sources) in their own countries. But in these countries Canadian history or Australian history was itself becoming isolated and introspective. Sometimes this was understandably (even inevitably) an expression of national self-assertion; often it was excessively narrow and parochial, even within its own national context, refusing at times with blinkered pride even to glance at comparative movements elsewhere, within the Commonwealth or outside. Strange local hybrids appeared. The Canadian studies programme developed a narcissism of in-look. Departments refused to consider candidates who had a degree from abroad as eligible. Associations of university teachers put barriers on foreign recruitment. Intellectually such interdisciplinary courses tended to attract the weaker candidates; and in history departments they seemed to encourage their faculty members to know more about less and less. Without intercommunication or synthesis they seemed to be impoverishing and ruining their own discipline. To quote a distinguished Canadian Professor, it left 'so little for the mind'.

Nevertheless, we stuck to our post and a wider view. Commonwealth history in Oxford still retained a unity which other universities cast aside. Some Indian and African historians still came regularly: others more fitfully and at Jack Gallagher's and later 'Robbie's' parties of course they flooded in from the outposts. We continued to try on Friday mornings to build around the specialisms of theses a broader framework of imperial history over four centuries and all continents, and to teach new research workers to use sources critically and with understanding. When Gallagher, offended by Balliol and drawn by Trinity, returned to Cambridge and — after another caretakership — in 1971 Ronald (Robbie) Robinson, that other great 'collaborator' (or, if you prefer, the other end of the Cambridge pantomime horse), came to the Chair, we tried to continue in the same course. Whereas in other universities, and even in this university in other areas of history, new research workers came in from outer space often to plod a weary and lonely furrow with sometimes only an occasional word with a supervisor, Commonwealth history has still, I think, a friendly welcoming face.

What other changes have occurred during the thirty years since Coupland retired? In 1950 the Readership in Colonial Administration created for, and filled with such distinction by, Margery Perham became retitled Colonial Government, at Kenneth Robinson's prompting when he succeeded to it (he wanted to be rid of 'Colonial' too but was defeated by Ralph Furse's claim that this would be too much for the morale of the Colonial Service). Nevertheless he gave the post a new dimension, not only wider than Margery Perham's concern for British colonial Africa, but also notably embracing the French experience, though that might have seemed to pose more of a problem when in 1956 the title was again changed to Commonwealth Government. So we stamp an office with a new look. When I followed him as Reader, I had frankly to tell the electors that, given the proximity of decolonization, my own interest would be predominantly but not exclusively historical, an emphasis not then (perhaps even now) entirely agreeable to Nuffield.

When David Fieldhouse followed me as Beit Lecturer in 1958, he was determined not to step only in my footprints: of course he inherited, and showed enthusiasm for, the responsibility for teaching the whole colonial experience from the seventeenth to the mid-twentieth centuries; but, not least under the influence of Max Hartwell, he struck away in part from my own constitutional obsessions to economic themes and sought with firm discipline and fine analytical mind to give some rehabilitation to the word 'imperialism' which Hancock had said rightly no scholar should use. When Colin Newbury succeeded George Bennett he sought to build a bridge from Africa (West, East and South) to the Pacific and went off in the steps of migrant populations. Similarly after my Directorship, the Institute of Commonwealth Studies — always misnamed, for it had never concerned itself with other than the tropical colonies and new states — came under a succession of development economists: a discipline where many in Oxford have made pioneering contributions. In the 1960s Margery Perham and I, with initial support from Nuffield College and inspiration from Sally Chilver and Bill Williams, launched the Colonial Records Project from its base at the Institute: its success in saving the papers of retired colonial administrators and others litter the Rhodes House basement and attract many scholars from Britain and overseas.

What then might be claimed, tentatively and with humility, as a special Oxford contribution to the empire-Commonwealth? We shall be considering any claim a specifically Oxford school might have made to the understanding of Commonwealth history; the first Oxford foci of imperial interest in India, the Indian Civil Service and Institute; the generous benefactions of the Rhodes Trust; the almost mystical vision of Lionel Curtis; Margery Perham's pioneer work on African administration and her devotion to the ideas of Lugard and indirect rule; and Keith Hancock's impressive surveys, particularly of the empire's recent economic record. There are many other themes which could be developed but for which there is little time or space in this review: an account of the training provided for the ICS, for the Overseas Services, for the Foreign Service Courses, for Visiting Fellows at the Institute or at request for Pakistan, Kuwait, Ghana, the West Indies, or most recently for Hong Kong: for when the plea for help in training came, Oxford in Hebdomadal Council and the Committee for Commonwealth Studies was not slow to respond. Ralph Furse insisted to me at the time of my election in 1957 that such teaching was the paramount duty of the Reader in Commonwealth Government. Or again we could consider more deeply the part played by the Indian Institute or Rhodes House or Nuffield College as foci of interest in imperial studies. Oxford is indeed fortunate in having in Rhodes House, not maybe a shrine or a Chequers as planned, but a very special and almost unique instrument for the study of imperial history, though sadly some dissipation of its holdings to other dependent libraries like the Law Library has already taken place. But the special place of Oxford in Commonwealth studies, if any, cannot be assessed if we fail to notice what contemporaries in the other universities were doing and how they saw the Commonwealth idea. This external view is of vital importance in considering any Oxford contribution and will be reviewed in a report which Kenneth Robinson is currently preparing.

There's another influence which we should mention: Kenneth Wheare – Beit Prizeman, Beit Scholar, Beit Lecturer: a political scientist of distinction who never lost the historical dimension he had displayed when teaching for history papers in the late 1930s. In his book on *Federal Government* (1946) which Beveridge had encouraged him to write, the hour of decolonization in the 1940s and 1950s found its Bible – much, indeed, against Wheare's wish; for, unlike Curtis, he found no special magic cure-all in federal government; but many of the attempted and failed federations of the post-war period may be traced to the influence of his book. Wheare was dubious, amused, and somewhat embarrassed by this subsequent decade of fashionable federalism The collapse of so many federations, hastily put together, was as he expected. Throughout his half century in Oxford he remained more than a little cynically detached both from the various evangelical fervours of Curtis, Coupland, and Harlow and from the misuse of his own intellectual interest. His commitment was to disciplinary, not area, studies.

The 1970s are no part of our brief and too close for comment. But perhaps one short (and final) remark is possible. There are fewer members of this seminar and many fewer locals than there were even in the 1960s. In 1970 I supervised over twenty candidates for doctorates; after this summer I shall have none.[14] Fewer candidates do any imperial history in Finals, due in part to the increase in the number of options. There has been no Commonwealth paper in PPE for over a decade, and there have been almost no candidates for the M.Phil. in Commonwealth and American history for many years. Indeed I have little doubt that I will be the last Reader in Commonwealth Government. For the first time this year, 1979, the Friday morning teaching seminar on sources was suspended – only one person, a New Zealander, turned up. (However, there were six new recruits to Commonwealth history in 1980, and fourteen in 1981.) The original Bell and Morrell special, 1830-60, changed in the mid-1950s to a Harlow and Madden one, '1774-1834', which David Fieldhouse halved and strengthened. Recently he and Paul

Langford have cut it once more but built it more firmly into late eighteenth-century British politics where a gap had yawned. After almost half a century the Indian special on 'Great Britain and India in the age of Hastings' had disappeared and a new special devised by Dr Raychaudhuri had moved into the twentieth century with 'Civil Disobedience and Constitutional Experiments 1919–1931'.

For David Fieldhouse and Paul Langford to move into the metropolitan scene was indeed neat and satisfying. But the pressure for regional history had taken its toll. In order to control and prevent too much proliferation a hybrid further subject which retained a common core on theory (which some tutors do not teach) but permitted specialization on old Dominions, South Asia, Latin America, and Africa was knocked together as 'Imperialism and Nationalism'. It drew its clientele largely from the old constitutional documents option, as indeed all the further subjects did; but in the mass of these new options only a small proportion of finalists do any imperial history and it is from these that we must now in the main recruit. Intellectually this shift may be regarded as no loss, and indeed quite natural. But I am not alone in thinking somewhat dubiously of the content, some of the teaching, and much of the performance in this new further subject. Meanwhile the Commonwealth history seminar is endowed with much loyalty and shows much vigour for much of the time, and plenty of friendly banter and warmth without rancour. We recognize, and tease, the parade of the hobby-horses – present, indeed, of course in Coupland's or Harlow's day, but greeted then with overt respect, not ribald comment: not now – 'collaborators', 'peasants', 'economic imperialism', 'responsible government', etc. – we wait their appearance with mirth. Even the conspiratorial theory of government – that imperial history is made by charlatans, pimps, bawds, cozeners, 'the pin-striped brigade', the whole crowd of Ben Jonson's St Bartholomew's Fair – can sharpen our perception and by contrast our reaction and our perhaps wider understanding.

In looking back over the first half century of Commonwealth history in Oxford, is it possible to note a specific Oxford contribution to the subject? What would seem to emerge convincingly is that, whatever their own specialization in period or region, these Oxford historians sought familiarity within a much wider frame of reference. They knew the British political and administrative background as well as the history of their colony, or colonies: they strove to know other centuries than the most recent and to find out about other empires. They were committed to see their own chosen period or region against as wide a canvas as possible, to seek beginnings, parallels, contrasts, and changes. They wanted to see imperial history in its fullest processes of evolution: continuity and comprehensiveness were their watchwords. It was an approach which Smuts might have recognized as 'holist'.[15] This was true of all the Beit Professors from the pioneering Egerton to (and notably including) the polymath Gallagher: Harlow's inaugural elevated the concept into a principle of faith. Perforce, given the variety of subjects they taught or supervised, it had to be true of the Beit Lecturers. With colonial America, eighteenth- or nineteenth-century special subjects, the emergence of the Commonwealth, the governments and politics of the several Dominions and major colonies as their required teaching, they had to be generalists. The many other tutorial Fellows — Pares, Williams, Beloff, Bennett, Newbury — cultivated this wider perspective. Specialization was a valuable basis for comprehensive judgement: it was not an end in itself. Imperial history would lose much if it became thus balkanized.

There was also for the greater part of this period another mark of Oxford imperial history — a missionary fervour for 'Commonwealth'. Within the university and the curriculum its intellectual force derived more from the Christian humanitarianism of Coupland and Harlow than from Curtis. But as counsellors to imperial administration cadets and as would-be men of affairs it permeated their arguments. This does not mean that all shared their optimistic faith: Wheare and Williams remained detached; even Harlow's evangelism was curbed by disciplined scholarship. That faith barely survived into the mid-1950s. In reaction Oxford seemed to turn away from a philosophy of empire. The very secularization of imperial history, which released levity at seminars unthought of thirty years before, strengthened the resolve to discover and to understand what happened and how it happened: to see historical events as they appeared to the actors on the global stage at the time, rather than with eyes conditioned by retrospective foresight, theory, or theology. The approach in Oxford became pre-eminently pragmatic at a time when oddly enough elsewhere (and not least in Cambridge) there was a new emphasis on theory: a new commitment to find a single conceptual framework to embrace explanations of the phenomenon of empire. So, while others have tended to put back theory and even teleology into imperial history, Oxford has become liberated from dogma.

Yet nevertheless, though shedding its missionary role, imperial history at Oxford has retained its concern with the near contemporary. Commonwealth history seminars tend, perhaps following Seeley's dictum, to see 'politics as present history' and to be dominated (to the impatience of some) by the newer issues of the recent past rather than those long-debated on the seventeenth, eighteenth, or nineteenth centuries. But, whereas it would seem that few elsewhere working within the field now acknowledge the 'holist' approach to Commonwealth history,[16] Oxford still strives to keep that flame alight: not because it is unaware of changing fashion, but because there is still a strongly rooted conviction that a comprehensive frame of reference in historical depth illuminates and strengthens judgement.

Notes

(After I had delivered this paper I was pressed to say where I was, what I was doing, and how did I know, which I hope excuses the autobiographical tone of some of these footnotes.)

1.   W. Blackstone, *Commentaries on the Laws of England* (Oxford, 1765–9).

2.   H. Merivale, *Lectures on Colonization and Colonies*, delivered before the University of Oxford in 1839, 1840, and 1841 and reprinted in 1861. This was again republished in 1928 by the OUP, at the same time as Bell and Morrell's *Select Documents on British Colonial Policy 1830–60*, for the purpose of teaching the new colonial special subject in Finals. Kenneth Bell wrote a brief introductory note.

3.   John Fell was Dean of Christ Church from 1660 to 1686.

4.   Max Beloff, *Imperial Sunset*, vol. I *Britain's Liberal Empire, 1897–1921* (London, 1969).

5.   Bill Williams took me to my first meeting of the Ralegh Club in 1938 to hear Lothian speak. He saw to it that I did my duty for a period as Senior Member of the Club when in 1957 I was elected to the Readership.

6.   Coupland was nominally my supervisor for the D.Phil. but, though we met regularly when I was in the Rhodes House Library, I think we only discussed my own research on three occasions. Bill Williams, who had supervised my B.Litt. on New Zealand after Richard Pares had had a brief spell of responsibility in helping to focus my research, was effectively my supervisor, mentor, and friend and has remained so with Kenneth Wheare (whom I had known closely from his time as lecturer on the same staircase in Christ Church) in all that I have written since. Coupland and Harlow were my D.Phil. examiners in 1950; Coupland and Pares had examined my B.Litt. – with an audience of two country parsons eating sandwiches at the back of All Souls Old Library to get out of a downpour.

7.   Colin Dillwyn of Christ Church supervised my reading for the Colonial Special Subject in 1937–8. There were no tutorials in special subjects at that time: reading was recommended and 'Collection' papers were set in college to test what had been done. Colin died in the war. Keith Feiling, who had been a Round Tabler in the early years, was at Christ Church but concerned himself with looking after those who chose the Indian special subject: from which interest came his later book on Hastings.

8.   He seriously contemplated leaving his house as a residence for future Beit Professors; but there were difficulties and it was clear that Harlow, so evidently his successor, would not leave his house in Old Marston.

9.   Harlow was more withdrawn than Coupland: he seemed to find social

occasions a burden, perhaps because they reduced distance and he was curiously aware of rank. He had a Pygmalion complex about his pupils and his 'staff', sincerely convinced that he knew what was best for them and for their careers. When faced, unconsulted, with transportation to chairs in Montreal and Adelaide, it was to Bill Williams and Ken Wheare that I went for understanding and support.

10. And the many undergraduates included future Commonwealth prime ministers – of Australia, Barbados, and Fiji for example.

11. Harlow lectured weekly in two terms on imperial history from the mid-eighteenth to the mid-twentieth centuries. In Trinity Terms he chaired discussions among members of the Courses on such questions as: in the light of historical and contemporary development is a multi-racial Commonwealth a practicable proposition? Does the British record support the criticism that the British have attached undue importance to political rather than economic development? Is it morally right for Britain to abandon the protection of race minorities in order to satisfy the claims of the majorities to independence? Is parliamentary democracy too alien to be successfully adopted by non-European peoples? Is it ever justifiable to sacrifice the rule of law to political expedience? or such motions as: 'The rate of progress towards self-government in British Africa has increased, is increasing and ought to be diminished.' 'Self-government is preferable to trusteeship.' 'Though Britain sought colonies in the past for the expansion of trade, no serious problems would result if she relinquished her colonies.' 'Security has always been preferable to opulence.' 'History shows that the formation of an integrated nationhood is impossible in a plural society.' etc.

12. When Richard Pares returned from the Chair in Edinburgh to Oxford in 1950 for an interminable decline from multiple sclerosis, John Bromley and I took turns in pushing his invalid chair from his father-in-law's (Powicke's) house to the lectures he gave each year on eighteenth-century America – lucid and amusing till the very end when he had movement only in his lips and eyes and neck.

13. The Beit Chair had been offered to J.C. Beaglehole but he felt he had to decline it. It should be pointed out that this assessment of Jack Gallagher stands exactly as it did before he died. This Oxford view of his time away from Trinity in Siberian exile is in no way modified by the obituary in the *Journal of Imperial and Commonwealth History* (June 1981): individually and collectively we owe him a great debt. I knew him as a fellow History Awarder for the Oxford and Cambridge Board in the early 1950s. When external examiner for the Tripos, I was privileged to see the Great Collaborators at work almost at the moment of gestation of the *Imperialism of Free Trade* (*Economic History Review* (1953)). On one evening in the late 1950s three successive Beit Professors present and future (Harlow, Gallagher, and Robinson) were at the Commonwealth history seminar and at dinner in Balliol afterwards.

14. In 1971 in the Commonwealth history seminar we had (in addition to Indian and African specialists many of whom were supervised by us non-specialists) research students in Canadian history ranging from the pre-Conquest to the Second World War, several in Australian and South African history, and individuals working on colonial America, New Zealand, Fiji, Jamaica, and Malta.

15. W.K. Hancock, *Smuts* (1962), vol. I, chapter 15.

16. It would seem, for example, to have been totally repudiated at a recent conference in July 1981 on the *diaspora* at Canterbury by settlement colony historians: none of the Oxford Commonwealth history team, however, were able to be present.

2 OXFORD IN IMPERIAL HISTORIOGRAPHY

Ronald Robinson

In his account of imperial history at Oxford, Frederick Madden suggests the rise and fall of a tradition — perhaps of a school which, beginning with Reginald Coupland in the 1920s and ending with Vincent Harlow in the 1950s, believed in certain values, and cast the subject into certain classic unities. From that time onwards the golden age appeared to darken; 'vandals' invaded from the Fens, desecrated the old beliefs, and overthrew the traditional unities, leaving the subject in disarray. There is much to be said for this point of view; its rich local colour is attractive, but the standpoint is also artfully contrived to provoke discussion of the broader issues that run through these essays. What ideas, for example, *have* imperial historians used from time to time to give unity to their writings, not only at Oxford, but elsewhere? Was there something characteristic, perhaps unique, about Oxford's classic conceptions? Was there, or indeed, *is* there a distinctively Oxford school of imperial history? These may be delicate questions for a 'vandal' to treat in the presence of Sir Edgar Williams, who has a right, if not the inclination, to speak for the local tradition. With his forbearance, they will be approached here, with a mixture of Oxbridge prejudices, through a set of personal reactions to the old masters.

The unities that have given imperial history whatever shape it has had during the past hundred years are so well known that they have rarely been defined or appraised explicitly. 'Mercantilism', 'expansion', 'organic empire', 'economic imperialism', 'Commonwealth', and the more recent 'excentric' or 'peripheral' notion — the stock of ideas looks remarkably unsophisticated when examined critically. They derive mostly from simple analogy with a mechanical, a biological, or a geometric principle. It is as if the imperial historian has pulled discrete aspects of various national histories unfolding on different continents into a unified field of study with a collection of mixed metaphors. Even so, each allegory has stood for a peculiar concept of empire, a particular analysis of the imperial process. Each offers a different definition of imperial scope and substance, a different scale of value for the judgement. One after the other, they originated in reaction to a profound alteration in the character of the contemporary empire. Each eventually inspired a new style of writing imperial history; but by that time the empire had changed its nature once again, turning the metaphor into an anachronism. It is necessary to review the development of these unities one by one, with the issues which Freddie Madden has raised in mind.

Historians of seventeenth- and eighteenth-century empire once defined their subject in terms of 'mercantilism', a notion which identifies the extension of colonial rule with the establishment of economic monopoly overseas. The pursuit of world power and the acquisition of wealth were assumed to be reciprocal in function and co-extensive in area, and this identification of the imperial state with the expanding economy would have provided the neatest unity for an imperial historian, had it corresponded with reality. Once Adam Smith had set up the idea for an 'Aunt Sally', however, and British trade with the United States continued to grow in spite of the downfall of colonial rule, the early Victorian economists formulated the converse of the mercantilist theorem, and divorced the expanding economy from the empire of rule.

The idea of 'expansion' which dominated the theory of the early and mid-Victorians, was conceived as an essentially economic process, stemming from industrialization, capital accumulation, and the international division of labour. They were all 'Marxists' in this sense, or rather, Marx was merely another mid-Victorian. While the colonial empire might come into this notion as an auxiliary, it was not regarded as a normal function of economic expansion. Although British settlements were planted overseas under the flag, colonial rule here was thought of as a temporary arrangement leading to local self-government and, perhaps, independence. And, though the interventions of imperial power became increasingly necessary to promote commerce, theoretically the trader and investor no less than the colonist was supposed to make his own way through contracts with the entrepreneurs of the rest of the world. According to this definition of expansion, Gibbon Wakefield, for example, could still describe the United States as British 'colonies' in the economic sense: the Indian Raj, on the other hand, could be dismissed in theory as an anomalous mercantilist survival. So far as formal empire was admitted into the conception, it was the 'kith-and-kin' empire joined to the 'mother country' not by *imperium*, but by what James Stephen in 1859 called 'tacit alliances' of free trade, free institutions, and religious toleration. The insignificance attached to the imperial state in the concept of 'expansion' is remarkable. The empire of rule seemed but the melting tip on the iceberg of expanding economy; and, so long as this unity prevailed, there appeared to be no significant empire to write about. Accordingly during the first three-quarters of the nineteenth century no specifically imperial history was written.

The empire of rule had to be abstracted from the wider notion of expansion and given a meaning in its own right before imperial history could become a unified field of study. Sir John Seeley, Regius Professor of History, turned this trick at Cambridge when, with encouragement from Florence Nightingale, he published his lectures on the *Expansion of England* in 1883. It was the only seminal idea in this field to come thence for many decades. Although Seeley, who previously had filled a chair of Latin in London, was no imperial historian, his flair for turning historical clichés into aphorisms delighted the rising imperial federationists and this book sold 75,000 copies within the year. As his editor, G.W. Prothero, claimed, 'He brought together . . . and regarded from one imperial point of view . . . imperial occurrences which historians had previously treated in a disconnected manner.' In presenting three centuries of British expansion culminating in an imperial federation, Seeley had reinvented the idea of formal empire as an 'organic' whole. His empire was organic in two senses: one, in insisting that the home islanders and the colonists overseas belonged to a single imperial nation (Australian 'Diggers' and Canadian lumberjacks were as much a part of it as the ratepayers of Kent or Cumberland); the other, in proclaiming that the 'sacred' destiny of the imperial nation could only be expressed in the extension of an organic imperial state.

His imperial organism nevertheless was by no means coterminous with the real empire. Though French Canadians and Afrikaners might be turned into Englishmen at a stroke of his pen, Seeley, like most of his contemporaries, could not do the same for Hindus, Muslims, or Africans. Non-European societies under despotic rule, imperial or otherwise, seemed to him by definition 'inorganic' and historically insignificant; and so India and tropical dependencies had no great place in his vision of a recentralized super-state.

The Regius Professor dismissed the British capitalist and merchant no less abruptly from his empire; for Seeley's ideal was designed partly to revive insular patriotism by extension to the empire overseas and partly to advertise the new university history courses as schools for statesmen. Neither object, he believed, was to be served in studying the dubious ethics of economic behaviour; and so his imperial organism had no economics. In this sense the previous definition of expansion had been inverted. The imperial state projected from London became the be-all and end-all of the process; the melting tip became the solid iceberg. None the less the organic idea provided the first academic historians with a unified study and defined the infant subject in one way or another up to the 1920s.

This particular organic concept became the stock-in-trade of Milner's Kindergarten and the early Round Tablers; the young Lionel Curtis became its Oxford prophet, while Hugh Egerton, first Beit Professor there, studied colonial policy and imperial federations in its light. The idea of an imperial nation, if not of an imperial state, inspired the imperial studies movement, including A.P. Newton, the first Imperial History Professor in London, who planned the *Cambridge History of the British Empire* published in the 1920s. These tomes stand as the classic historiographical monument to the Seeleyan unity of organic empire. Contributors fixed their gaze on imperial policy, constitution-making, and administration, and on the projected activities of British government, as if the organic imperial state had actually come into being to do everything of significance in these countries, while their indigenous inhabitants slept. Though each dominion is given a volume, implying that they might have some history of their own, even here the imperial connection is kept to the forefront, while two volumes devoted to India are filled with accounts of its official administration. The tropical dependencies, vastly enlarged since Seeley's day, were also presumed inorganically to have no history except that given them by their rulers, and were treated under general imperial policy in the first three volumes. Long before Hugh Trevor-Roper declared that Africa had no history, the Cambridge editors had decreed that it should be so. Their standpoint was anglocentric and their values Anglo-Saxon, although there was much of value in their pioneer narrative. The possibility that the empire drew its power from the periphery no less than the centre, from the subjects as well as the rulers, never occurred to these writers. Economics and informal empire were left almost entirely out of the account.

Meanwhile John Hobson, the radical publicist, had published his book on *Imperialism* in 1902. Though he revived the earlier notion of economic expansion, he brought it back into the strait-jacket of Seeley's imperial state. To make a historical case for redistributing domestic wealth more equitably, this secular moralist found the 'tap-root' of the Boer War and the recent African and Chinese partitions in surplus capital looking for higher profit through the annexation of new empires. Later, in the hands of Russian and German communists the notion was sharpened into a doctrine of 'imperialism' as the fatal stage of finance capitalism. Hobson's idea of economic imperialism proved unfortunate from the historiographical point of view. He had borrowed

Gibbon Wakefield's capitalist analysis of the earlier colonies of British settlement to explain the newly acquired tropical empire in Africa and elsewhere. The right formula had been applied to the wrong empire. More than that, the Hobsonians restricted the operation of economic imperialism to the period after 1870, excluding the settlement colonies, whose existence the economic explanation had been designed originally to explain. Error was thus compounded.

According to this idea of economic imperialism the extension of the empire of rule manifested a capitalist invasion of Africa and Asia. Whereas Seeley had dismissed the tropical colonies as politically in-organic, at least they could now be thought of as economically organic; they were none the less viewed as simple projections of British political economy for all that. The standpoint remained exclusively anglo-centric. But it was in the field of values that the idea of economic imperialism had greatest effect. Hobson and his successors had con-founded the politics of empire with the economics of capitalism in a double condemnation. Eventually this moral challenge set off the debate over motives, over degrees of moral intention and economic self-interest behind imperialism which has occupied the subject to this day. The controversy has usually been conducted on such simple assumptions as to become almost as futile as that which once raged over the question of Bismarck's sincerity. But the theory of economic imperialism was too unpatriotic or anti-imperial to influence imperial historiography in British universities much before 1945. Outside their walls, however, between the wars, the radical Leonard Woolf used the notion in his critique of empire and commerce in Africa, as did Leonard Barnes and others; but the vogue took more hold in the United States. There, H.E. Barnes edited a score of volumes on dollar diplomacy in South American banana, sugar, and nitrate republics: Leland Jenks, Herbert Feis, and J. Fred Rippy produced their studies of capital export; and Parker T. Moon, his *Imperialism and World Politics* (1926) – all in the frame of economic imperialism. The impact of the idea was largely polemical. Anti-imperial nationalists everywhere adopted the manifesto against exploitation through domination, and hence the idea of capitalist imperialism contributed more to the breaking of empires than to the unities of academic historiography.

Turning next to the idea of 'Commonwealth', which during the inter-war years played a large part in rebutting the charge of economic imperialism, we come at last to Oxford and the question of a great tradition. By that time the dominions had evolved into independence and free association in a white Commonwealth; dominion status for

India was coming into view; nationalists in many other dependencies were grinding against colonial rule, and the empire was beset with problems of race relations. Yet no new general idea had been introduced into imperial history writing since 1900. Academic detachment had emptied the subject of theory and reduced it to the chronicling of disconnected themes. A new unifying concept was not to be looked for from Cambridge where the first Vere Harmsworth Professor, Admiral Richmond, was taken up with naval, and his successor, Eric Walker, with South African history; nor from London, where Newton studied 'areas' with his pupils, while Professor Lilian Knowles concentrated on local economic developments with hers. If the unities of imperial historiography were to be re-established, Oxford would have to supply them, not only because the study had matured longest there and her historians were less 'scientific' and more 'philosophical' than elsewhere; not only because they were most involved in policy-making and reflecting the issues of the day in writing more contemporary imperial history; but also because, to outsiders at least, they seemed to be typically Oxford ideas. That is not to say they were invented or patented there, but Oxford brought them into historiography in a characteristic form and style.

These unities of the golden age clustered round the ideal of a multi-racial Commonwealth to come. It was to come from a vast improvement in imperial ethics, from substituting the more enlightened principles of trusteeship, 'indirect rule', and the 'paramountcy of native interests' for those of the old racial empire of 'kith and kin'. On these assumptions the history of empire tended to be analysed not so much as a governmental or economic process, but as a moral progress; an education, however prolonged, preparing subject peoples for entry into a family of nations no longer exclusively Anglo-Saxon, but embracing all races. The allegory became one of an empire of shepherding dependencies through time into self-government and dominionhood. According to this unifying idea the empire-Commonwealth was criticized and justified as a single moral organism working increasingly on the side of the angels in history.

Lionel Curtis, as Deborah Lavin shows in her chapter, was the original recruiting sergeant, and in some ways the archetype of this school of imperial historiography. As the second Beit Lecturer in colonial history at Oxford, founder of these Friday seminars, and later as a Fellow of All Souls, the 'Prophet' used his history to preach imperial federation *before*, and multiracial Commonwealth *after*, the First World War, attracted Coupland from ancient, and Hancock from Italian history to the cause. Curtis was the first Round Tabler to break the colour bar of the white Commonwealth, when in 1917 he preached responsible government on the Canadian model for the Indians and their eventual inclusion in an imperial federal government. Later, on the same federal model, he helped prescribe 'dominion status' for Irish, and 'dyarchy' for Indian nationalism. In all this the 'political mechanic', as he described himself, typified Oxford's faith in the genius of British imperial institutions to reform political human nature wherever they could be transported. His faith reached so far in the end as to discover the embryo of world government in the empire-Commonwealth. There some, but not all of the Oxford school, followed him. Nevertheless, the spirit of Curtis's *Civitas Dei* shines at no remote distance through their work. This kind of Christian idealism is perhaps the distinctive feature of these classic unities to which Freddie Madden has referred.

If Curtis was the John Bunyan of the empire's moral progress, Reginald Coupland might be regarded as its Gibbon, except that, like Curtis, Margery Perham, Nicholas Mansergh, Keith Hancock, and Vincent Harlow (but unlike Gibbon), Coupland was a convinced Anglican. In his inaugural lecture of 1921, the second Beit Professor defined the unities which were to inspire Oxford's imperial historiography for the next three decades. He found the 'answer of history' to the 'demon of an overweening nationalism' which, he believed, had caused the late war and now threatened to disrupt the empire, in the 'twofold ideal of freedom and unity'. 'The ideal', he contended, '*has* been realized, the problem of nationality *has* been solved, in more various ways, and on the largest scale, by the political society . . . we have learned to call the British Commonwealth.' Here was the moral organism *par excellence*, and his noblest achievement was to bring the Indian and dependent empires into its historical scope. Coupland prophesied that the Commonwealth ideal would solve the 'problem of race' which he regarded as the other menace to empire and world peace. 'If the political association between Britain and India becomes . . . a genuine comradeship yoking Europe and Asia in free service to their common weal,' he believed, 'the longest and hardest stage will have been accomplished . . . toward the brotherhood of man.'

Coupland chose his themes and wrote their history with this ideal in mind. The moral of his lectures on *American Revolution and the British Empire* (1930), for example, was that 'We lost our American colonies . . . because we . . . never made a real constructive effort to solve "their grievances".' The moral drawn was the tragedy of schism within the British community. In his studies of the Quebec Act of 1774 and the Durham Report of 1839, the principles of racial equality and colonial self-government, combined with the lesson of American federalism, point the way to the Commonwealth of 'multinational federal states' of his own day. The problem of nationalist schism was thus resolved. The same constitutional formula, he thought, should have settled the Irish question; and in *The Empire in these Days* (1935) and *The Indian Problem* (1942-3) he gave the Indian nationalists historical reasons why the Commonwealth formula should also settle their racial difficulties within the empire. By 1936 he could acclaim an India Act that granted them 'a measure of self-government roughly corresponding to that of the dominions in the penultimate stage of their advance' to independence. Coupland's history, like Curtis's polemic, read back into the imperial past the gradual but inevitable triumph of Commonwealth institutions and ethics.

Coupland's history not only brought India into this unity but extended it to Africa and the dependencies elsewhere. Here, as Freddie Madden has suggested, he drew his inspiration from the Victorian humanitarians with their insistence that all races were equal before God and should be treated as such. He wrote best perhaps on Wilberforce, on Kirk on the Zambesi, and on the crusade against slave trade and slavery in the dark continent. At the end of his study of the anti-slavery movement, Coupland acclaimed 'one of the three or four perfectly virtuous pages' in history which expiated 'the greatest imperial crime against humanity'. The evangelists on behalf of other races were his real heroes from Buxton to Livingstone, Gordon, Kirk, and latest, and most surprisingly, Lugard. They represented in his work the empire of moral force working in history to atone for the racial sins of the old imperialism and justify the righteousness of the new. Coupland's evangelical tenderness towards subject races inspired one of the earliest accounts of indigenous African history in his study of the pre-colonial East coast. It ends with an invocation to his ethical empire — 'bringing the East Africans out of the darkness into the life of the civilized world . . . in which they would be treated no longer as living tools for other peoples . . . but as peoples as much entitled as any other . . . to lead their own lives for their own ends'. The ideal of multiracial Commonwealth required for him an improved and improving standard of imperial trusteeship and interracial justice. 'In the age-long contact between the diverse races . . . between white and coloured, between strong and weak,' he wrote, 'imperial rule must become a means of mutual understanding and co-operation rather than of conflict and oppression.' 'Whatever its character in earlier days, our Imperialism must . . . come in the end to mean an honest attempt . . . in our treatment of the weaker peoples . . . to fulfil the common need for freedom and unity on earth.' The moral unity of the empire-Commonwealth in his historiography was thus perfected.

It was perfected for Coupland so far as the African empire was concerned in Lugard's principle of indirect rule and in the ethic of native paramount interest. The one had become largely identified with the other during the 1920s when, as Hancock sourly observed, African colonial problems were treated as simple problems in applied ethics. Curtis and Coupland took their stand with Lugard, Cameron, and Oldham against the Kenyan and Rhodesian settlers' claim to the privileges of the old 'kith-and-kin' empire through self-government in a great white dominion. The advocates of interracial equality in Commonwealth preached the extension of West African standards of trusteeship to East and Central Africa as they had come down from Mary Kingsley, E.D. Morel, and Lugard and so the priority over settler interests of native development through indirect rule became another characteristic tenet of the Oxford school. It enabled Coupland to bring Africa into the multiracial 'meaning and purpose' of the empire-Commonwealth as a whole. 'Africans', he wrote, 'are beginning in their own native forms a similar process of assimilation or equalisation as that now consummated in the nations of the Commonwealth and nearing its consummation in India. . . . A Dominion of Nigeria? Why not?'

During the 1930s the unities which Coupland had defined were extended to the colonial administrative history of Africa in Margery Perham's pioneer studies, as Anthony Kirk-Greene's chapter in this book shows. Her *Native Administration in Nigeria* (1937) helped swing the gaze of imperial historians away from the theory of policy in Whitehall and Westminster to the actualities of executive work in the field, and so brought out the essential collaborative connections between colonial and indigenous African authorities for the first time. Like the rest of the so-called Oxford school, she wrote near-contemporary history with current colonial problems very much in mind, arguing the case for continued imperial trusteeship in the South African High Commission territories, and insisting on native paramountcy in East Africa with equal moral and historical conviction. The alternative, she warned, correctly as it turned out, was 'to drift towards a particularly dangerous and insoluble type of racial politics'. She began by recording the practices of 'indirect rule' in the districts and ended by erecting them into a kind of historical theology. Just as Curtis and Coupland had given the Indian nationalists historical reasons for fulfilling their aspirations within the Commonwealth, so Margery Perham found historical reasons for believing that indirect rule would advance Africans to the same dignity, at the same time sparing them and their rulers that phase of brash, unrealistic nationalism which afflicted India. 'The whole object of indirect rule', she proclaimed, '. . . was to train people in self-government.' Most colonial administrators used this policy in practice for purposes of frustrating the emergence of nationalism and consolidating imperial control. In fact when the time came to take self-government for the African dependencies seriously, after 1947, there was to be no possibility of constructing it out of confederated local native authorities on indirect rule principles. So much for the lessons of imperial history. For Dame Margery as for Coupland, however, indirect rule was more than an administrative method or even an education for self-government; it was a moral principle, the only approach to race relations in Africa worthy of the name of trusteeship. At least the doctrine called for a measure of justice and freedom to the ordinary African in protecting his indigenous organization and, with it, his ownership of the land and the fruits of his labour from European capitalist or settler expropriation. By attaching historical means to ideal ends in this way, the Oxford historians brought the African empire alongside the Indian into the historiographic unity of the multiracial Commonwealth.

It was left for Keith Hancock to consummate and transcend these Commonwealth unities which had become established at Oxford, in a history on the grand scale. They found their most individual and sophisticated expression in his *Survey of British Commonwealth Affairs* published between 1937 and 1942. As Deborah Lavin shows in her chapter in this book, the work was commissioned by Chatham House which Curtis had founded, and Hancock acknowledged his debt for unifying ideas not only to him but to Arnold Toynbee and Alfred Zimmern with whom Hancock and Curtis shared the fellowship of All Souls. It is not surprising therefore that the first volume of his *Survey* bears some of the hallmarks of the so-called Oxford school. Typically the past is reviewed as background to current imperial problems, according to the multiracial values and teleology of an emerging Commonwealth. Though Hancock made as if to criticize these unities, he nevertheless proclaimed that 'The British Commonwealth is nothing else than the "nature" of the British empire defined in Aristotelian fashion by its end,' and went on to shape its history into a dialectic between *Imperium et libertas*, culminating triumphantly, if with difficulty, in the 'liberty, equality and fraternity of self-government and racial impartiality'. Nothing could have been more orthodox, although less weight than usual was given to the imperial, and more to nationalist points of view. Like Coupland and Perham he 'tried to get at the roots of specific problems in specific territories' without denying 'the real unity that permeated the (empire) Commonwealth even in its diversity'. Like them also he focused on race relations which were making the 'procession' of dependencies 'to the finishing post of self-government' 'ragged here and there'. His accounts of Africa were formulated on their principles of trusteeship, native paramountcy, and indirect rule; for example, in his criticism of the Empire Resources Development Committee's projects for colonial exploitation, of European and Indian pretensions in Kenya, his approval of Lugard and the West African tradition of native peasant production which denied palm forest concessions to Leverhulme. Lastly Hancock was typical of Oxford in his concern to repel the challenge of Leninist and Stalinist doctrine to Commonwealth values; but here he departed from his predecessors into economics. 'Since [the] basic postulates [of anti-imperial theory] were economic,' he wrote, '[he] could hardly claim to have tested it seriously without studying the processes and policies of production and distribution' of investment and marketing within the empire-Commonwealth.

Because Hancock was an economic as well as a political historian, and an Australian, but above all because Hancock was Hancock, when he extended the traditional unities to the economic aspect, they were transcended in a new cosmology. Imperial historians up to this time had viewed their subject largely from the standpoint of constitutions and administration exported from Britain. More than that, the various elements in the working of imperialism had been studied hitherto in separate compartments; economic aspects had been monopolized by anti-imperialists or pure economic historians, the politics of the centre had been appropriated by patriotic imperial historians, while those of the peripheries at the other end of the process had been left to colonial historians. In the last two volumes of his *Survey* (1940, 1942) Hancock became the first historian to articulate the separate parts in synthesis. By combining Turner's frontier theory of American history with the idea of European expansion, he was the first historian to connect the moral, economic, and political drives from the centre comprehensively to their social impact on the satellites and dependencies overseas. His distinction lies not so much in his economic history, as in his analysis of the interaction of projected wealth, power, and religion in the various indigenous conditions of the missionary, trader, settler, and planter frontiers. Few economic historians today would preface an inquiry into 'men, money and markets' with the question 'What had Christian evangelism to do with economic policy?' But for Hancock as for the classical economists, secular and religious, morality and market, inter-racial equality and land, liberty and labour were all dimensions of each other in a historical no less than a philosophical sense.

Nicholas Mansergh may be regarded as the last representative of Oxford's ideal Commonwealth school, though he professed the subject mostly in Cambridge after the Second World War, and, like the others, gave its by now old-fashioned unities an individual twist, a more con-temporary reference. By the time of his *Surveys of Commonwealth Affairs*, from 1931 to 1952 (two volumes, 1952, 1958), the ideal, so far as India and a few Asian dependencies were concerned, seemed to have been accomplished. The British 'club' had opened its doors to non-European members. Mansergh could indulge soberly in the vindication of Oxford's *civitas dei*. 'As I travelled round the Commonwealth,' he wrote, 'I took to heart the Psalmist's injunction: "Walk about Sion . . . mark well her bulwarks . . . and tell them that come after." ' But if the spirit was the same, the manner in which he did so was different in some respects. Mansergh did not try to bend the Ulysses bow of Hancock's comprehensive analysis. There was no more economics in his account than Seeley would have wished and, as Mansergh focused his attention on the story of co-operation between Commonwealth members, the dependent empire dropped out of his picture. For him, as he explained in *The Commonwealth Experience* (1969), the ethic of Commonwealth was not only distinct from, but utterly opposed to, the ethic of empire. Freedom was the principle of the one; subjection, the principle of the other. Accordingly, the dependent empire was excluded from his teleology. By that time there was no dependent empire to be justified, so that the idea of empire-Commonwealth as an organic moral unity which Coupland and Perham had stood by could be rejected out of hand. Mansergh's view of Commonwealth history narrowed to one of international relations between independent members and those parts of their individual histories connected with them. Hancock's successor thus broke the central unity of the great tradition.

Though all these historians used the ideal of Commonwealth in one form or another as a frame, their individuality in other respects leaves the case for bringing them together into a distinctively Oxford school open; but they were certainly admired and criticized as such from the standpoint of Cambridge in the early 1950s. In Ifor Evans, who published his *British in Tropical Africa* in 1929, 'the other place' had had its theologian of indirect rule before Margery Perham. Hancock's *Survey* inspired George Kitson Clark to insert a paper on the expansion of Europe into the historical tripos there in 1945, chiefly to give ex-service undergraduates something easy to read. Clive Parry, E.E. Rich, and Jack Gallagher lectured on the subject among others, and Cambridge booklists acknowledged Oxford's ascendancy in near-contemporary imperial history during the inter-war years. Yet, as Mansergh found on arriving in Cambridge in 1956, and Gallagher was to find when he came to Oxford in 1963, the unities established in the two universities were not easily interchangable. The Oxford unity of 'Commonwealth' and the Cambridge unity of 'expansion' proved so far apart in their assumptions and values that it might seem the one was virtually untranslatable in the idiom of the other. It is this mutual incomprehension which is perhaps the best evidence of a peculiarly Oxford 'Commonwealth' school.

In Cambridge at least the Oxford style seemed unmistakable; the high moral tone, the lofty view which Mansergh called 'largeness of mind' and Hancock 'span'; the penchant for tracing philosophical antitheses through long historical perspectives, for presenting the imperial record teleologically in terms of an ideal end. In the fenland climate, where philosophy was linguistic and secular scepticism poured on religiosity, the Oxford imperial tradition seemed to offer more faith than science. By 1950 the 'vandals' felt that Oxford's 'Liberal Anglican School' had gone too far in preaching from historical facts that the empire, like the Commonwealth, was 'C. of E. and a good thing'. Few beside the Cam believed in Commonwealth as a unified field of historical study; it was considered but part of the wider processes of expansion. Oxford's historical method seemed 'unhistorical' in Cambridge, where it was not done to preach values through the past or to present it marching inexorably through selected themes into a better present and future. Butterfield had taught Cambridge to suspect such 'Whig interpretations'; Oxford's imperial historians seemed to take pride in them.

If these criticisms were to some extent justified, they applied not only to Oxford where some of the most significant innovations in the subject had been achieved, but to imperial historiography everywhere before 1950. The inter-war years may have been the golden age of inspiration, but they might also be regarded as the dark age of anachronism, archival poverty, and confused analysis. Considering the unities discussed so far, their logical defects are as impressive as their effect on interpretation was distorting. They were founded more on beliefs than researches. With each of them a patriotic or moral ideal was imported from the present into the past, which as a result tended to be surveyed as background to current imperial problems on a priori assumptions, rather than investigated as a chronological process. At a time when many archives were not yet opened, the philosophical approach was perhaps unavoidable; nevertheless, once they were opened up it became questionable whether the unities employed up to 1950 were historical unities at all; they were imposed on the materials more than they arose out of, or were demonstrated by, them. Each of them had led historians to mistake a part of the empire for the whole and generalize it to the wrong parts at the wrong time. The idea of economic expansion, for example, was transferred by theorists of economic imperialism from the early settlement colonies to the Afro-Asian empire which it fitted least. The notion of the organic state was applied by Seeleyans, not to the empire of rule, but to the self-governing Dominions which it suited least, giving an impression of an empire of rulers without subjects; while the ideal Commonwealth of the future was projected backwards (chiefly by Oxford historians) into the interpretation of Indian and African empires in periods when their rulers had no serious intention of relaxing control in order to achieve it. Yet, for all the misappropriation, each of these unities isolated a vital element in the imperial process, which, when used as hypothesis rather than dogma, would lead eventually to consideration of all the rest. Once again a change in the contemporary reference brought about a new perspective and gave rise to a different synthesis.

By the early 1950s the end of Europe's colonial empires was in sight. British expansion had ceased long since: American and Russian expansion was overtaking the rest of the world by other means. As the Marshall plan showed, Western Europe with its remaining dependencies had fallen, potentially at least, into dependence on the United States, and British imperial historians could appreciate expansion for the first time from the receiving end. It is not surprising that informal empire took on a new meaning for them at this time, or that they began to reappraise the history of formal empire in its light. The empire which had once seemed a monolithic projection of British power in Asia and Africa now appeared to have been a gimcrack hegemony over indigenous authorities always on the verge of xenophobic or nationalist overthrow. Hence the possibility that imperial rule had drawn its force more from the collaboration of its subjects than from exported power could no longer be ignored. The old anglocentric unities began to crack.

In Oxford the transition to a more scientific historiography was marked by Vincent Harlow's publication in 1952 of the first volume of *The Founding of the Second British Empire, 1763-93*, one of the first objective expressions of a multi-faceted unity in imperial historiography. Though he inherited Coupland's faith in Commonwealth along with his chair, and had propagated it from the Ministry of Information during the war, Harlow's interpretation was not distorted by idealism. Rather than study current imperial problems in the past, he studied the past itself, inducing his synthesis from deep research, as a comparison of his book with Coupland's lectures on the American Revolution and the British Empire will show. Coupland had traced the empire-Commonwealth's genius for reconciling nationalists through institutions of freedom in unity, to the lessons of the American Revolution embodied in the Quebec Act and the Durham Report. Harlow rejected his teleology as unhistorical. The statesmen who designed the reformed colonial system, he declared, were not 'gifted with second sight', and could not have foreseen that 'the American demand for self-government was a challenge that would be repeated from Toronto to Colombo'. For Grenville in 1791 the Canada Act was the only sensible expedient for preventing the spread of republicanism to the remnant of British North America, while Durham's Report of 1839 at the time was merely an appendix to the Reform Act of 1832. Harlow interpreted the imperial record through the eyes of the actors at the time rather than through the hindsight of the present.

He went on to attack the Stubbsian legalistic view of imperial history which had been in vogue previously. 'The history of Britain's relations with her colonies', he proclaimed, is not simply 'a matter of devising constitutional machinery to satisfy the aspirations of colonial nationalism but also of "social divergence" and specific calculations of interests on all sides at specific times.' Contrary to the Seeleyan view, 'The second Empire' which he discovered 'was a predominantly coloured Empire ruled not through representative institutions, but a strong bureaucracy directed from London.' Though his viewpoint never moved far from the anglocentric, his fascination with the strategies of the central official mind led to more sophisticated appreciation of different kinds of British empires and the discrete processes making and breaking them in different regions. The third Beit Professor was thus able to write the history of something 'that was not an empire', as he put it, 'in the normal sense', but which held several sorts of thraldom together in interaction. This led him to make what was perhaps his most influential innovation. From studying the diverse processes he discovered 'the general principle' governing all of them in the preference for trade over dominion of which much was soon to be made in Cambridge. In this he became the first imperial historian to take 'informal empire' fully into account and relate it through local crises to the contraction and expansion of the empire of rule. The idea was not an act of faith: the principle was induced experimentally from Shelborne's abortive proposals for the settlement of America and Ireland and from an analysis of the 'swing to the East'. It was the fruit of investigating imperial expansion as he felt it must be studied 'concurrently in the country of origin and in the distant regions affected'. In that sense Harlow after Hancock was among the first to employ a more sophisticated unity in which several elements and standpoints of empire were combined; and after all, the art of the subject lies in the synthesis.

In Cambridge the reaction against the pre-war anglocentric approach brought about by the falling of empires and the making of new ones was carried on similar lines to a more radical definition in the so-called 'excentric' idea. Gallagher and Robinson's manifesto of 1953 on 'The Imperialism of Free Trade' owed something to Hancock, not a little to Harlow, a great deal to apprehension of the colonial possibilities in the Marshall plan, but most perhaps to a socialist and agnostic reaction against the patrician Anglican complacency of the distinguished Oxford Commonwealth school. The Cambridge writers, finding themselves in an ethical quandary between Coupland and Perham's moralization and Hobsonian and neo-Marxist denunciation of British imperialism, took up scientific method and, fixing on the question of imperial motives, tried to account for the timing of extensions and contractions of the empire under Queen Victoria. A paradox entangled them in the existence within the same empire of a strategy which liberated its most valuable settlement colonies while annexing many more less valuable tropical dependencies. The contraction in the one case ought not to have happened on the theory of economic imperialism; the expansion of rule in the other seemed inexplicable on any anglocentric view, as no compelling motive for acquiring more tropical empires could be found at the centre. Nor would the paradox go away so long as the empire of rule was treated as a self-explanatory entity. It became necessary to broaden the inquiry beyond the red on the map to include informal empire, asking why it modulated sometimes in some areas into formal empire, but not in others; and why, at other times in other places, formal modulated into informal once more. A hypothesis was set up to resolve the problem, in which local and indigenous factors outside Europe largely determined imperial intervention or withdrawal and decided the nature of empire in different regions. 'The type of political lien between the expanding economy and its formal or informal dependencies', it was suggested,

> has varied with the strength of their political structures, the readiness of their rulers to collaborate . . . the ability of the native society to undergo economic change without external control, [and] the extent to which domestic and foreign situations permitted [imperial] intervention.

In this way the early Victorian idea of expansion with the political dimension added was tied to reactions at the receiving end; the anglocentric organic concept had been reversed.

Imperialism was soon defined in Cambridge as a set of reflex actions between European and extra-European components. 'From Europe stemmed the economic drive and strategic imperative to secure its gains against rivals in world politics.' But these components, according to the excentric notion, took the form of empire only when they operated at cross purposes with the extra-European component of indigenous collaboration and resistance. On this assumption empire was to be considered a product of almost random interactions between wealth and power projected from Europe and autonomous change and continuity in the domestic history of other continents. Hence imperialism could no longer be regarded as a systemic process, being a true function neither of the expansion of Europe, nor of the indigenous history outside Europe. It had become 'excentric' to all of the cycles of history involved. The courses and character of empire appeared to be shaped more by subjects on the periphery than rulers in the metropolis; empire became the mirror image of xenophobic nationalism; anti-imperial nationalism the mirror image of empire.

To claim for this notion, as some in the Fens have done, that it brought about a historiographical revolution is to claim too much. Certainly the idea completed the demolition of the traditional unities which Hancock and Harlow had begun, and also emptied the subject of Commonwealth values; but, as Jack Gallagher would have said, the notion came from reshuffling earlier concepts, changing trumps and dealing a fresh hand. The idea of collaborating élites, for example, was suggested by Perham's work on indirect rule. Excentricity, however, was not designed for the purpose of unifying exposition but as an experimental hypothesis, which has made the writing of any comprehensive imperial study a more arduous task. At least Gallagher and I, the authors of *Africa and the Victorians* (begun in 1951 and completed ten years later), had reason to think so; even though that work, like Harlow's, was organized on the unity of the official mind at first, the excentric notion soon arose out of it and this Frankenstein monster has pursued them ever since. Not until the early 1970s was the idea realized in a comprehensive imperial history, and then ironically at Oxford with David Fieldhouse's *Economics and Empire, 1830–1914* (1973), though by that time in Cambridge it had inspired several monographs by the 'Indian school' of Gallagher and Anil Seal, and not a few on collaborative systems in colonial Africa and informal empire in South America. At its most constructive perhaps the excentric idea provoked controversy, a rethinking of basic assumptions; and yet, for all their contempt for previous Whig interpretations, in perpetrating the 'peripheral' principle Robinson and Gallagher were no less guilty of anachronism. They had projected the fall of empire in their own time, the triumph of nationalist subjects over waning rulers backwards into the interpretation of earlier empires which could hardly have been established and upheld without strong central power. In this sense the idea has proved a better unity for analysing new nationalism than for accounting for old empires.

Which then was the golden and which the dark age of the unities at Oxford? There is perhaps no answer to that question. No one university can file patent on any of these unifying ideas, since they were the common stock of contemporary reference. They evolved like the English language, out of triangular intercourse between London, Oxford, and Cambridge, and, more recently, with American and Commonwealth universities, particularly in India and Africa. Fortunately, when it comes to blowing ideas through trumpets, all halls of learning are one. The quality of the history written depends not so much on the merit of the unity employed, as on the historian's willingness to abandon it, if it will not work, in favour of a more sophisticated definition. The subject has languished in single-minded isolation and flourished with the variety of standpoints and ideas exchanged. During the inter-war years the Oxford school made an outstanding contribution to the evolution of the contemporary Commonwealth, but the golden age of its ascendancy would have been dark for the subject had not Cambridge advanced another idea. It is necessary for the survival of the subject that its unities should be continually broken and recast.

Fifty years hence the historiographer will look back and say that the subject was still in its infancy today, waiting for the dust to settle on the downfall of Europe's empires to bring the necessary detachment. He will probably be more impressed than we are by the force of the expansive centres than by the peripheral rigidities of imperialism, considering that the centres since 1960 have regularly projected more wealth and power on the rest of the world in a single year than was exerted throughout the nineteenth century. In formulating this situation, our successors may well find the organic unities of the Victorians and Edwardians more realistic than the peripheral theories of the 'New Elizabethans', and conclude that, for all the imperialism previously recorded, the history of expansion only began in earnest in the mid-twentieth century. If that is so, the golden age of the subject in Oxford and elsewhere is yet to come.

3 OXFORD AND INDIA

Richard Symonds

The connection between Oxford and India was so long, and its strands
so various, that it is hard to know where to begin. It could be in Christ
Church, with its long line of portraits of Governors-General, and where
the movements for the conversion of India were launched; or in Balliol,
where in the 1880s half the Indians in Oxford and half of the Indian
Civil Service (ICS) probationers in Britain studied; or in the old Indian
Institute, the elephants and deities on whose walls remind us of high
hopes and a scandalous misappropriation of the building. But it seems
suitable to commence in the Church of St Mary the Virgin, where a
boss of Mahatma Gandhi looks down on a massive memorial to Sir
William Jones, ambiguously surmounted by what may either be an
Oxford Ox or a Brahmini Bull, not because Jones spent long in Oxford,
but because of his seminal influence on Indian studies there.

There had, of course, been contacts between Oxford and India long
before Jones. Hamayun Kabir, lecturing at his old university as Minister
of Culture of Independent India in 1960, even courteously maintained
that from the end of the sixteenth to the end of the eighteenth century
Oxford had been the most important single factor in bringing India and
Britain nearer to each other in the field of knowledge. He instanced
the Jesuit Father Thomas Stephens from New College, who in Goa at
the end of the sixteenth century wrote an epic poem in Mahratti to
convey the lessons of the Old and New Testaments; the books of the
East India Company (EIC) chaplains, Edward Terry and Henry Lord,
on Indian language and customs in the seventeenth century; and the
Bengali Grammar of Nathaniel Halhed in 1778.[1] These, however, were
isolated individual contributions, whereas Jones was to establish a
tradition of Oriental Studies not only in Oxford but in Europe.

Oriental Studies

Jones, who lived from 1747 to 1794, had the broad interests of a scholar
of the Age of Enlightenment; whilst an undergraduate at University
College, he brought in a Syrian to share his rooms and teach him
Arabic, and he used manuscript material in the Bodleian to study

Persian. In London he was a member of The Club and friend of Samuel Johnson and Burke, before he went out to Calcutta as a judge of the Supreme Court, with the two objects of studying Sanskrit and of saving enough money to be able to devote the rest of his life to scholarship. In his eleven years in India he saved £50,000 but died as he was about to re-embark for England. His greatest achievement was to demonstrate the genetic relationship of Sanskrit to the major European languages, and it would be hard to overestimate the importance of this for the future of oriental studies and the Indian cultural renaissance. He also investigated Indian botany, astrology, and music, and made digests of both Hindu and Muslim law.

In 1832 Colonel Boden of the East India Company endowed a Chair of Sanskrit at Oxford with an annual stipend of £1,000 and tenable for life; 'being of the opinion that a more general and critical knowledge of the Sanskrit language will be a means of enabling his countrymen to proceed to the conversion of the Natives of India to the Christian Religion'.[2] The first holder of the Chair, however, Horace Hayman Wilson, was less inspired by the vision of the conversion of India than by the work of Jones. Almost as versatile, in a different way, he had gone out to India as a surgeon; and had been Master of the Mint whilst taking up Sanskrit studies. In 1823 he had persuaded the Bengal government to strengthen existing Hindu and Muslim colleges, and encourage publications of Indian literature and learning. Before returning from India to Oxford Wilson was the leader of the Orientalists in their losing battle against the Anglicists, Macaulay and Trevelyan, over whether government funds should be devoted to education in the English or oriental languages.

Wilson only resided in Oxford for three weeks a term as Professor, simultaneously holding the post of Librarian at East India House. However, he published the first dictionary of Sanskrit in any language, published and translated Kalidasa, and brought Max Mueller to Oxford.

On Wilson's death a celebrated and uninhibited election campaign for his chair took place in 1860 in Convocation between Max Mueller, broadly supported by the Liberals and Reformers, and Monier Williams, backed by the Conservatives. *The Times* commented that, whilst Monier Williams was a competent Sanskrit scholar, Max Mueller was 'simply the greatest Sanskrit scholar alive'. Monier Williams's supporters suggested that Max Mueller's nomination was part of a plan of the Prince Consort to place 'a whole array of German Professors, spectacles on nose and pipe in mouth, in possession of our cloisters'. The protagonists of Max Mueller spread rumours that Monier Williams did not understand Sanskrit, but the country clergy's vote carried the day for Monier Williams. The consequence was a tragedy for Oxford. Max Mueller, bitterly wounded, turned from Sanskrit to philology and comparative religion. His contribution to these fields was great, but his enmity to Monier Williams encompassed the Indian Institute.[3]

Max Mueller and Monier Williams were the dominant figures in Indian studies in Oxford in the second half of the nineteenth century. They were almost exact contemporaries. Max Mueller was the son of a librarian and poet in Dessau, Germany; he studied Sanskrit in Berlin and Paris and then came to England in 1846 because the East India Company, at the instigation of H.H. Wilson, undertook to finance publication by the Oxford University Press of his edition of the *Veda*. Settling in Oxford to oversee this work, he lectured on modern languages and comparative philology, was naturalized, and became a Fellow of All Souls. After his defeat in the election for the Boden Professorship, a Chair in Comparative Philology was created for him by the university.

His influence went far beyond Oxford. Not only did he do much to establish Sanskrit as a third classical language, but he introduced and popularized the study of both comparative language and comparative religion. He was a frequent lecturer to the Royal Family. A thousand copies of one of his sets of lectures were sold on the day of publication, and a major undertaking was his organization of the publication by the Oxford University Press, at the expense of the India Office, of a series of Sacred Books of the East.

Max Mueller was not enthusiastic about the increasing number of Indians who came to study in Oxford in the 1880s. He considered that they often returned with inappropriate and anglicized values. He cared much more for the fostering of an Indian renaissance and wrote:

> By encouraging a study of their own ancient literature, as part of their education, a natural feeling of pride and self-respect will be reawakened among those who influence large masses of people. A new national literature may spring up, impregnated with Western ideas, yet retaining its native spirit and character.[4]

Oxford's role, as he saw it, rather than shaping Indian students to the model of English public school gentlemen, was to train Englishmen to go out to India and help in the creation of Indian institutions. To do this he continually argued for the strengthening of the study of Indian languages.

Max Mueller was a Lutheran. Because of his ecumenical philosophy, he had to defend himself against charges of being lukewarm towards missionary activity. In doing so, he proposed that the university give financial support to missionaries who would serve as correspondents or 'Cultural Vice-Consuls' in addition to carrying out pastoral duties.[5] Nothing unfortunately came of this imaginative suggestion.

Overshadowed by Max Mueller, Monier Williams's reputation has not stood high in recent years. He had considerable handicaps to overcome. His father, who was Surveyor-General of Bombay, where he was born, died when he was a child. He entered Balliol, but, before taking a degree, moved to Haileybury to prepare for service with the East India Company. His brother's death in action in India caused him, for family reasons, to decide to remain in England. He returned to Oxford, where Balliol did not take him back. At University College he overworked and was awarded a double fourth class degree. He went back to Haileybury to teach Sanskrit. When Haileybury closed, the Boden Professorship was a providential opening, and he admitted to spending £1,000 on the election.

Describing his own main quality as 'plodding perseverance', Monier Williams spent twenty years in establishing the Indian Institute in Oxford. His objects in doing so were, firstly, to provide a centre for union and intercourse for all engaged in Indian and oriental studies, including scholars, administrators, and distinguished Indians; secondly, to provide a means of restoring the *esprit de corps* of Haileybury for the ICS probationers; and thirdly to promote the welfare of Indians in Oxford, whether matriculands or merely residents.[6]

Starting indefatigably in 1875, he obtained approval and a site from Congregation; he collected money, with a subscription list headed by the Queen, and visited India to obtain moral support from the government and lakhs of rupees from maharajahs. The foundation stone was laid by the Prince of Wales in 1883. The Institute opened in 1884, and the building was completed in 1896.

Max Mueller would have nothing to do with this project. He circulated a flyleaf to Congregation, urging that the funds collected should be spent on research and fellowships rather than buildings.

'What all the Indians say', he wrote later, 'is that the rich Oxford University went round with a hat, promised to help Indian students at Oxford, and all the money they subscribed in India was spent on bricks and stuffed animals.'[7]

At the laying of the foundation stone Jowett, as Vice-Chancellor, described the Institute as 'a sign of mutual interest and affection between Oxford and India for many centuries'. We could only safely govern India if we knew it, he said; 'there was a great debt which England and Europe owed to India, though it might be one to be paid in the far distance'.[8]

Thirteen years later, at the formal opening, Lord George Hamilton, Secretary of State for India, expressed qualms that the ICS, who were so admirably performing their work, were not increasing in popularity on the scene of their labours. The Institute could constantly remind the ICS probationers of the great Indian civilizations; that when their ancestors were unclothed savages there was a literature and architecture in India well worthy of being preserved; and that there was a need for closer and more sympathetic relations between English and Indian peoples.[9]

These hopes were hardly fulfilled by the Institute. Lord Curzon, who visited it as Chancellor of the University in 1909, criticized its conception as 'too grandiose'. Its social gatherings had fallen into disuse. Its museum collection, so painfully accumulated by Monier Williams, he described as 'of no service to education, and equally useless to art and science'. 'That it is visited annually by more women than men', he observed, 'is a sufficient condemnation of its retention here.'[10]

It never became, as planned by Monier Williams, a hall of residence for Indian students; nor, as Max Mueller hoped, a centre of research. Its main activity was the course for ICS probationers, which lacked the cultural impact envisaged by Lord George Hamilton and Jowett. After the ICS course ceased at Independence, Congregation and Convocation, after spectacular debates and accusations of bad faith towards maharajahs, decided by a narrow majority that the building should be taken over by the university for administrative purposes and the Library removed to the New Bodleian. This, as was pointed out in the debates, happened just as Cambridge was establishing a Centre for South Asian Studies. By a final irony, the building, stated by the Hebdomadal Council to be too frail to support the weight of its books, is now the library of the History Faculty. It is only fair to add that the Indian Institute Library remains the best open-shelf library on the subject in this country, even though the carelessness with which the portraits and other objects were disposed of may be considered a lamentable reflection of Oxford's lack of interest in Indian history.[11]

The work of the later Boden Professors has been succinctly described in the brilliant inaugural lecture of the present incumbent, Professor Gombrich, in 1977. Monier Williams's immediate successor, MacDonnell, acquired for the Bodleian the largest collection of Sanskrit manuscripts outside India. Berriedale Keith did useful cataloguing of these Sanskrit papers early in the twentieth century. However Gombrich concluded 'we are not very good at English; we are not very good at Sanskrit, and we are not very good at anything else', and was appalled to find that no Indian had ever been employed to teach Sanskrit at Oxford or at any other British university.[12] As for other languages, G.U. Pope deserves special mention. He was the leading Tamil scholar of his time, and Jowett made him Chaplain of Balliol.

The Conversion of India

Because the majority of Oxford's graduates and teachers were in Holy Orders until the middle of the nineteenth century and even later, it was natural that the conversion of India to Christianity should have been a subject of recurring interest.

As early as the 1680s Fell, who was Bishop of Oxford and had been Dean of Christ Church, persuaded the EIC to support four or more scholars annually at Oxford to study Eastern languages and divinity and become chaplains of the Company. Fell also arranged for translations and printing by the University Press of the Gospels in Malayan. Neither initiative was very fruitful. The chaplains became too busy looking after their European congregations and in trading on their own account to devote much time to evangelization; nor were Malayan Gospels of much use in Bombay, Madras, and Bengal. Moreover, by Aurungzeb's reign the company was on the defensive and its policy became one of excluding Christian missionaries.[13]

In 1813, the Company was obliged by parliament to admit missionaries to its territories. In the Oxford University Archives considerable interest in the conversion of India can be found about this time. Thus in 1804 the Rev. Claudius Buchanan offered a prize to be awarded by the university for the best work in English prose on 'The probable design of the Divine Providence in subjection of so large a portion of Asia to the British Dominion, the Duty, the means and consequence of translating the scriptures into the oriental tongues, and of promoting Christian knowledge in Asia'. Despite the Vice-Chancellor's support, Convocation rejected this offer, but in 1840 it accepted a prize given by an official of the EIC for

> the best refutation of Hinduism, together with a statement of the
> evidences of Christianity as may be most suitable to the mental and

moral character of the learned Hindus, including those facts which the perverted conditions of the Hindu intellect and its want of historical information may render indispensable.

It is in this context, as we have seen, that the Boden Professorship of Sanskrit was endowed in 1832.[14]

To Reginald Heber, who was Bishop of Calcutta from 1822 to 1826, it never appeared that the conversion of India would be an easy task. Heber had been one of the most distinguished students of his time at Oxford, winning the principal prizes for Latin verse, English poetry and literature, and becoming a Fellow of All Souls. Strongly influenced by Sir William Jones, he wrote that 'A missionary needs to be a scholar and a man of cultivated mind, for in many of his hearers he will meet with a degree of knowledge and refinement which a parochial minister in England does not often encounter.'[15]

Travelling widely, and recording all aspects of Indian life, he criticized the rudeness of the company's officials, contrasting this with the memories left by the French, 'who, though often oppressive and avaricious, had a great advantage over us in the easy and friendly intercourse in which they lived with natives of rank'.[16] Heber would invite Indians to dinner, and his wife would present them with pan and rose-water when they departed.

Oxford provided a number of Evangelical clergy to India in the mid-nineteenth century. Among the most notable were Daniel Wilson, Fellow of St Edmund Hall, the first Metropolitan of India, who as Bishop of Calcutta from 1832 to 1858 attacked the Indian government 'for showing favour to Mahommedanism, countenancing the gross abominations of Hinduism', and not permitting religious instruction in schools: and there was T.V. French, Fellow of University College and first Bishop of Lahore, who was, like other pupils of Dr Arnold, never able to relax, and after retirement died of heatstroke whilst seeking to convert the Arabs of Muscat.[17]

The university's most ambitious contribution to the conversion of India, however, came later in 1880, when the Oxford Mission to Calcutta was founded in Christ Church by Talbot, Gore, Liddon, and Scott Holland, all leading high churchmen. This was in response to an appeal from the Metropolitan of India, who called upon the university to provide men to work among the students of Calcutta. The Oxford Mission was – and remains – a celibate order, which claimed that 'if not officially, yet definitely and distinctly it represents Oxford to India. Through it the University of Oxford ministers of its intellectual and spiritual wealth to the deep poverty of the University of Calcutta.'[18]

Just as early Christianity had spread through Jerusalem, Antioch, and Rome, so it was argued that in India the critical point was Calcutta, its administrative and intellectual centre. On the Hindu side the Brahmo Samaj appeared to the first superior of the mission, the Vice-President of Cuddesdon, to provide a monotheism which could lead to Christianity. As for the Muslims, Father O'Neill, another of the first members of the mission, believed that 'All Muhammedan nations are dying out through their own vices'.[19]

Rapidly the Mission established a hostel in Calcutta for students who, coming from lower-middle-class Bengali village families, often lived in great poverty and squalor. The Christ Church connection caused the hostel to be named 'The House' and its yard 'The Meadow'. Its only rule was 'that those living in the home must behave like gentlemen'. A magazine *Epiphany* was specially directed at students, for discussion in correspondence columns of religious, literary, and social questions. By 1898 the Mission had established a complete system of boys' education from village school, industrial school, high school, university boarding house to theological class.

And yet, as early as 1889 a certain disappointment with the results of the dialogue with the educated classes became apparent.

An Englishman [one of the fathers wrote home sadly] will not readily open his mouth on a religious subject, but if he does, he means it. The Bengali is always ready to talk about religion, but then one discovers that his interest is only intellectual and superficial, and that nothing is further from his thoughts than to accept responsibility for such truths as he is lead to acknowledge.[20]

By 1910, as the Hindu revival developed, it was admitted that 'the class which we hoped to influence are harder to guide towards the faith because they are now largely given away to political ideals'. The sights began to be lowered. 'Though the work has not led to direct conversion such as we hoped,' one of the fathers wrote in the Mission's history, 'indirect results have been obtained in the Christianisation of thought and character among those who are still not Christians.'[21]

About this time the Bishop of Calcutta somewhat surprisingly diverted the main effort of the Mission to Barisal, a remote area of East Bengal where a few thousand Christians, who had alternated between the Baptist and Episcopalian churches, needed pastoral care.

The flow of Oxford recruits dried up and in later years the fathers came mainly from Cambridge and London.

Yet the Oxford pioneers who served longest, Father Douglass of Christ Church, a moderate scholar but a good oar, and Mother Edith, who had been Vice-Principal of Lady Margaret Hall, left a vivid memory of the last flare of the Oxford movement. Their first priority was prayer, daily prayer for the conversion of India; educational and other good works never took precedence over this. Secondly, they sought to work through Indian Brotherhoods and Sisterhoods, which should as soon as possible become independent, living according to the principles of the rule, but each with a separately adapted constitution and way of life. Thirdly in Calcutta, and in Behala on its outskirts, they provided a rare atmosphere in which the Bengali middle class — ridiculed, despised, and feared in British official and commercial circles — could discuss intellectual problems freely with British graduates.[22]

There was little in the high church atmosphere of the Oxford Mission or of the Cowley Fathers, who worked in Bombay, of the tolerance of other religions or of Indian aspirations and culture shown by Jones and even Heber. Father Benson, Superior of the Cowley Fathers, compared the Taj Mahal unfavourably to Keble College,[23] and Father Douglass, a privileged eccentric at the age of eighty, even after Independence, removed a portrait of Netaji Subhas Bose from the hostel walls and hurled it in the fire.[24]

The Indian Civil Service

The Committee on the Indian Civil Service in 1854, of which Macaulay was chairman and Jowett a member, trusted that under the system of competitive examination, which its report introduced, the ablest graduates of Britain's universities would be recruited. In 1861 twenty Oxford graduates were successful, but in 1864 the maximum age limit for competing was reduced from twenty-three to twenty-one. The effect was not only to discourage Indian candidates but to leave the field in Britain largely to men who, after leaving public schools, spent two years with a crammer. In 1866 62 per cent of the successful candidates had no degrees, and by 1877 the proportion had risen to 79 per cent.[25]

In 1878 Lord Salisbury further reduced the maximum age limit of candidates to nineteen years, but made a two-year probationary period at one of eight universities in Britain obligatory after the entrance examination. In 1892, under pressure both from Indian public opinion and from the British universities, the age limit was raised to twenty-three years, and at the same time the marking system was brought more into line with the curriculum and practice of Oxford and Cambridge — especially Oxford.[26]

No one took a keener interest in the association of Oxford with the ICS appointments than Jowett, as Master of Balliol. They would, he said, provide an answer to the dreary question which a college tutor so often hears: 'What line shall I choose with no calling to take orders, and no taste for the bar, and no connections to put me forward in life?'[27] 'The advantages to university education of a share in Indian appointments', he wrote to Gladstone, 'are almost incalculable. You love Oxford too much not to do what you can for it.'[28]

Jowett wrote to every successful ICS entrant offering him a place at Balliol, where in 1879 more than half the probationers in the country were studying,[29] and Arnold Toynbee was appointed as their special tutor. The university regulations were adapted to allow them to substitute Arabic and Sanskrit for Greek and Latin, and to take a degree in two years.

One reason for Jowett's enthusiasm was the importance which he attached to the influence of Oxford on men who were destined to hold high office. As he wrote to his former pupil, the Viceroy, Lord Lansdowne, in 1888, 'There is more opportunity of doing great and permanent good in India than in any department of administration in England.'[30]

But there was another reason for Jowett's desire to attract not only ICS probationers but Indians to Oxford. He had suffered severe humiliations in the struggle for university reform; he had been summoned by the Vice-Chancellor to reaffirm belief in the Thirty-nine Articles; he had been refused his professorial stipend; and he had lost the first contest for the Mastership of Balliol. Now that the reformers had won, they were divided between those led by Jowett, who considered that the university's main task was teaching, and those, led by Mark Pattison, who wished to place the emphasis on research. In the promotion of oriental studies both factions could combine. By bringing the majority of the probationers to Oxford, Jowett induced the India Office to provide funds for more staff. When he became Vice-Chancellor he made a list of priorities, at the top of which was the establishment of the Indian Institute.

When the age limit was raised in 1892, the *Oxford Magazine* published a series of articles drawing the attention of tutors, particularly in Greats, to the advantages of the ICS as a career. The editor pointed out that the pay and prospects far surpassed those of the home service and that an ICS officer might even prudently invite a girl without a penny to marry him. The inducements were effective. Between 1892 and 1896 52 per cent of successful candidates were Oxford graduates.[31]

Until the First World War there were few Indian entrants to the ICS. After 1918 the pattern changed. Indian candidates recruited from Oxford and Indian probationers became an important element under the Montagu-Chelmsford reforms, by which 50 per cent of places in the ICS were reserved for Indians. On the other hand between 1918 and 1939 the number of successful British candidates varied according to the economic situation and conditions of service. In some years British officers had to be appointed by nomination in order to maintain the British quota.

A sufficient number of probationers, British and Indian, came to Oxford to enable the course to be maintained until the Second World War. The probationers were attached to colleges, and the Indian Institute provided only teaching and library facilities. Hunt and Harrison's materials, collected from ICS survivors, give the impression that for the British in later years the course was 'a bit of a lark', not very useful except in respect of Indian law and languages, though even the latter often turned out to be inappropriate. For the Indian probationers, however, about to serve a British Raj, the acquaintance with British life and institutions provided self-confidence. Both British and Indian officers make the criticism that the cultural, historical, and economic background of the people among whom they were to work was neglected.[32]

The Effect of Classical Studies

An interesting area for research would be the effects of the Classical Moderations and Greats Schools on attitudes of British politicians and administrators towards India. Of the little that has been written, R.M. Ogilvie's *Latin and Greek* is most stimulating, though it does not deal primarily with empire.[33] Elphinstone said that no British official in India travelled without a copy of Thucydides in his pocket.[34] Ogilvie suggests that from their study of Thucydides British administrators bore in mind, among other things, the use of native troops, the preservation of existing institutions, and the exploitation of internal politics, characteristic of the Athenian empire.

This, perhaps, was more Haileybury's contribution than Oxford's in the first part of the nineteenth century. Under Jowett Plato's influence became more important. Inexpert intelligence was seen as the best quality to bring to government, and the virtues necessary for an empire were loyalty, courage, and responsibility. Ogilvie sees the Edwardian period as a Homeric age, in which there was a preoccupation with honour rather than morality. Curzon might fit into this category, though perhaps he had Roman history as much as Greek in mind when he said that he could not understand how anyone brought up at Oxford in his generation could fail to be an imperialist. The classical influence persisted until the end. Sir George Cunningham, last British Governor of the North-West Frontier Province, told the students of St Andrews University that the study of Latin, with its hard logicality and economy of words, was the best foundation for a colonial administrator;[35] and Bandaranaike, who was to become Prime Minister of Ceylon, found permanent inspiration in Gilbert Murray's lectures on Homer.[36]

Prophets and Worthies

The men who influenced late Victorian Oxford most were Jowett, Ruskin, and T.H. Green. What they had in common was contempt for the results of *laissez-faire* and for the Manchester school. Jowett, who taught economics as well as philosophy, wrote in relation to India that 'ignorance and impatience of taxation may do a great deal of harm in an underdeveloped country, if it leads to discontinuance of public works required for health and education'. He advocated 'the need for instruction in India in agriculture and engineering and waterworks'.[37] Arnold Toynbee, whom Jowett appointed as tutor to the ICS probationers, was later described by one of them as 'one of the most brilliant exponents of the new humanitarian school of economists which was then battering against the frigid materialism of the Manchester school'.[38]

Ruskin had many messages. *The Stones of Venice* (1851-3) are reflected in the Bombay railway station. His imperialism was a race imperialism, urging young Oxford men to go out and settle in vacant lands, which hardly applied to India, in which he took little interest. When Monier Williams appealed to him to subscribe to the Indian Institute he refused, replying, 'Oxford, as I understand its position, has to educate young English gentlemen in the elements of noble human knowledge, not to prepare them as clerks in foreign counting houses'.[39]

It was Ruskin's insistence on the dignity of human labour, however, which, though in Oxford it produced the comedy of Milner and Oscar Wilde jointly and ineffectively straightening the road from North to South Hinksey, was to influence Gandhi to make his disciples spin cotton and clean latrines.

Prophetic figures were fewer in the twentieth century. There was indeed the Prophet himself, Lionel Curtis, who had some responsibility for the introduction of dyarchy into the Montagu-Chelmsford reforms. But his tactlessness caused an instruction to be issued that members of the ICS were not to take part in Round Table activities.

Sir Reginald Coupland, who was Beit Professor from 1920 to 1948, took an active part in Indian affairs as member of the Lee Royal Commission on the Superior Civil Service in 1923 and with the Cripps Mission in 1942. His books on the Indian problem were influential in official circles and he acted as a talent spotter in Oxford for the ICS. Though the blandness of his style may have been irritating, there was realism as well as rhetoric in his address to the Oxford Majlis Society in 1931:

> I am proud of what England on the whole has done in India in the last hundred years. But that is nothing to what my pride will be if England can help to bring this connection to its natural and noble climax and help to set India in her place, as a Dominion in our Commonwealth of Nations. . . . After the Round Table Conference there is no going back. You are the first generation of Indians to be called on to determine the destiny of India. . . . The democratic government of India is the hardest political task that any nation has attempted. What is the message which the spirit of Oxford, our Common Mother, so old and wise, has whispered to generations of her scholars in their hours of weariness and disappointment — nothing is worth doing that is not difficult to do![40]

The somewhat complacent view of colonial history which was later to cause Coupland to be savaged by Eric Williams of Trinidad was also gently rebuked by Gandhi at a meeting convened by A.D. Lindsay at Balliol during the Round Table Conference. Coupland was attempting to persuade Gandhi how British history showed that, with mutual patience and goodwill in working evolving constitutions, self-government gradually and inevitably emerged. Gandhi replied that he was only a simple villager and not a learned professor, but this was not how he read the history of Britain's relationship with America and with Ireland.[41]

For Oxford it was important that through eighty years there were influential members of the university who had extensive experience of the problems of Indian government. Sir Henry Maine used his experience as Law Member of the Viceroy's Council in his lectures on village communities, while he was Corpus Professor of Jurisprudence between 1869 and 1877. A little later W.W. Hunter, who had organized the *Indian Gazetteer* and first census, came to Oxford. Sir Michael Sadler, Master of University College in the 1930s, had been Chairman of the Calcutta University Commission, whose report was a massive analysis of India's educational problems. His contemporary, H.A.L. Fisher, Warden of New College, who married Ilbert's daughter, had been a member of an equally exhaustive commission on the public services in India. At All Souls, resident and visiting fellows in the 1930s included, in addition to Coupland and Curtis, two former Viceroys (Chelmsford and Irwin), as well as Simon, Amery, Curtis, and H.V. Hodson, all of whom were involved in Indian constitutional reforms.

Racial Attitudes

Another interesting area on which little research has been done is the influence of Oxford on racial attitudes. Of the nineteenth-century Regius Professors of History, Goldwin Smith was an anti-imperialist, but Stubbs, and still more Freeman and York Powell, with their enthusiasm for Anglo-Saxon, Norman, and Icelandic virtues, may have exercised an indirect influence on imperial attitudes towards coloured races. Froude was an imperialist, though not directly interested in India. In this area Jowett's impact on his pupils and former pupils was once more significant. Jowett deplored the fact that 'an Englishman cannot govern without asserting his superiority. He has always a latent consciousness of the sense of colour.' He saw the difficulty of India as social rather than political, and hoped that 'the Oxford education would provide a courtesy of manner in dealing with the natives of India'.[42]

The Cult of Duty

Somewhat separate from the evangelical strand is the cult of earnestness and duty which emanated from Rugby and Oriel. Thomas Arnold, who was Regius Professor of History as well as Headmaster of Rugby, insisted in his lectures that the object of the study of history was its moral lessons.[43] His son, W.D. Arnold, abandoned an Oxford career because he was out of sympathy both with high church and evangelicals, and went out to India as an officer in the East Indian Company's army, subsequently becoming Director of Public Instruction in the Punjab. In an autobiographical novel, *Oakfield*, published in 1854, he wrote that, 'The obvious work of every Englishman in India seems to me to be to justify his title to a position in a country not his own by trying to civilize it.' 'The Indians', he said, 'are a deplorably inferior race, but I do not consider them hopelessly so.' He successfully opposed the attempt of Sir John Lawrence to introduce compulsory Bible reading into government schools, because it offended his sense of fair play. W.D. Arnold was one of the earliest of a long line of Oxford men who became teachers or educational administrators in India.[44] Among the most respected was Sir Edwin Arnold, Principal of Poona College, whose poem on the life of the Buddha *The Light of Asia* (1879) had a huge circulation.

Anti-Imperialism

By the 1930s the anti-imperialist influence in Oxford was quite pervasive. One of its most effective proponents was Edward Thompson who, after service as a Methodist missionary in India, taught Bengali to the ICS probationers from 1924 to 1934 and then became Research Fellow in Indian History at Oriel. His books, *The Other Side of the Medal* (1925) and *The Rise and Fulfilment of British Rule in India* (1934), provided an intellectual base for the Indian policy of the Labour party. Thompson was contemptuous of the education system in which he had served in India and deplored the racial attitudes of most of the British who worked there, but he retained an unwilling admiration, and perhaps envy, for the decisive role of the ICS.

From their memoirs it appears that the majority of Indians who studied at Oxford in the 1930s were enrolled in the Labour Club, which became more Marxist as the decade went on. Palme Dutt was a frequent visitor, and G.D.H. Cole was an important figure both as its senior member and as a teacher of economics.

Oxford Historians of India

Oxford's professional teachers of Indian history were more interested

in the history of British rule than the history of India. They were also
more concerned with political and administrative than economic, social,
or cultural aspects. S.J. Owen, the first Reader, who held the post for
almost forty years from 1868, had previously spent a few years teaching
at Elphinstone College, Bombay. His first book on *India on the Eve of
the British Conquest* (1872) disclaimed any use of Indian sources, but
was full of references to the 'Moral Turpitude and Repulsively Low
Morality' of Indian rulers.[45] Britain's task, Owen considered, was to
civilize India before converting its population to Christianity. Wisely,
he later concentrated on editing the despatches of Wellesley and
Wellington.

Vincent Smith became Lecturer in Indian History on retirement
from the ICS in 1900. His books on early Indian art and history were
pioneer works. In Oxford, however, he turned to political history. His
massive *Oxford History of India* (1919) has been criticized because 'the
imaginative and intellectual effort demanded in order to see the world
through the eyes of a people not nurtured in the Bible and classics was
too much for him'.[46] Moreover his Irish Protestant origins caused him
to lose any objectivity when steps towards Home Rule — whether in
Ireland or India — were discussed; he chastised Gladstone and Ripon
and devoted a book to an attack on the Montagu–Chelmsford reforms
(1919).

Sir Verney Lovett, who was Reader in Indian History from 1920 to
1932, was another former ICS official. His scholarly reputation was
precariously based on his *History of the Indian Nationalist Movement*,
which was written in 1919 from an official point of view and dismissed
Gandhi as 'now an elderly man', when the latter was only fifty and had
still thirty years of political life before him.[47] Whilst at Oxford Verney's
main contributions were chapters on administration in the *Cambridge
History of India*, and lectures to the ICS probationers who seemed to
find them particularly tedious.

About the same time P.E. Roberts taught Indian history as a special
subject for thirty years, and wrote a lengthy *History of British India*
(1938). His predilections may be illustrated from his observation that
Vincent Smith had 'lightened and simplified the whole dreary and
repellent subject of the Hindu and early Muhammedan periods'.[48]

The main interest of C.C. Davies, who was Reader from 1936 to
1965, was Warren Hastings. His successor, K. Ballhatchet, did not hold
the post for long before resigning after the Indian Institute controversy.
Thus, with the notable exception of Edward Thompson, who held a
college, not a university post, it was only after Independence, with the

appointment of S. Gopal and T. Raychaudhuri, that Indian history was much studied from an Indian as well as a British point of view.

In the 1930s, Lord Lothian, Secretary of the Rhodes Trust, aware of the official orientation both of Indian history and of the courses offered to the ICS probationers at Oxford, persuaded the Trustees to offer to endow an annual visiting lectureship which would bring distinguished Indians such as Iqbal or Srinivasa Sastri to lecture on Indian history and culture in the university. Nothing came of his initiative, the file disappearing in a change of Vice-Chancellor.[49]

Anthropologists

Oxford probably made a more lasting contribution to the study of Indian anthropology than of Indian history. Several of the ICS officers who had studied at Oxford became eminent as anthropologists of India. Among them were Sir Herbert Risley (1851-1911), J.P. Mills (1890-1960), J.H. Hutton (1885-1968), and Sir Wilfred Grigson (1896-1949). All of them became interested in anthropology through their work with primitive tribes. Risley, Mills, and Hutton were Census Commissioners. Risley, whose book on *Tribes and Castes in India* (1891) was a pioneer classic, was the archetypal scholar-administrator, Home Secretary to the Government of India and President of the Royal Anthropological Institute. Both Mills and Hutton wrote books on the Nagas, which are still used as textbooks, and held academic posts on leaving the ICS — Mills as Reader at the School of Oriental and African Studies, and Hutton as Professor of Social Anthropology at Cambridge.

These scholar-administrators were often able to see the results of their anthropological approach to their work. Hutton successfully advocated clauses which protected primitive tribes in the Indian Constitution of 1935; and for twenty years the administration of Bastar proceeded on the lines laid down by Grigson as a result of his book on the Maria Gonds.

The Oxford Diploma Course in Anthropology, which was the first to be established at a British university in 1908, was the child of classicists, Gilbert Murray, Arthur Evans, and R.R. Marrett among them. The ICS anthropologists from Oxford had mostly read classics and tended to see Indian tribal society through Homer's eye, recognizing how ancestor worship determined laws of inheritance, and how minor Gods presided over boundaries, rocks, and trees: even the shape of a village courtyard would remind them how Penelope's suitors were trapped by Odysseus.[50]

Verrier Elwin (1902–64) came to India with a different background and made a different kind of contribution to Indian anthropology. After taking first-class degrees in English and Theology, he went out to India with the Christa Seva Sangha Mission, whose members lived in Indian style. His association with Gandhi and Congress caused him to become *persona non grata* with the administration, within which, however, Oxford friends saved him from deportation on condition that he confined himself to non-political work. He then settled among and wrote about the Gonds in Central India, doing social service as an act of reparation for what they had suffered, and marrying a village girl. Jawaharlal Nehru made him Adviser for Tribal Affairs after Indian Independence, when he took Indian nationality. So Elwin, too, became a scholar-administrator. In his memoirs he expressed his debt to Oxford for two important things: a love of poetry, which brought him to anthropology; and a neoplatonic philosophy which enabled him to endure the isolation and tragedies of village life.[51]

Indians at Oxford

The earliest Indians to appear on the matriculation rolls entered Oxford in 1871. Between then and 1893, forty-nine Indians matriculated. Of these twenty-two were at Balliol, eleven at other colleges, and sixteen were non-collegiate. In this period a high proportion were Hindus from Bengal and Bombay, and Parsees were well represented. But, somewhat surprisingly, in view of what was being written about the backwardness of their community in education at the time, over 20 per cent were Muslims. Only three of the forty-nine went into the ICS; about half became barristers.[52]

One of the first women students at Oxford was Cornelia Sorabji, a Parsee whose parents were Christians. From a very early age she determined to qualify as a lawyer, in order to devote her life to helping women in Purdah, who were often cheated of their rights and inheritance because they were unable to consult male lawyers. From the University of Bombay she won an open Government of India scholarship, tenable at a British university, but was disqualified from taking it up by her sex.

Lord Hobhouse, a former Law Member of the Governor-General's Council and keen supporter of women's rights, arranged for Somerville College to provide a substitute scholarship for her. Jowett, who had been Hobhouse's contemporary at Balliol, arranged for her to attend lectures in law at Balliol and All Souls, and, being Vice-Chancellor, persuaded Congregation to pass a special decree, enabling her to sit for the BCL examination in 1892, although she was only able to collect the degree thirty years later. Her work on behalf of Purdah women on her return to India was invaluable, and for many years unique.[53]

Between about 1905 and 1920 a number of Muslim students from Aligarh who were afterwards to play an important role in the politics of India and Pakistan were undergraduates at Oxford. Liaquat Ali, Pakistan's first Prime Minister, was at Exeter, studying law. One of his successors, H.S. Suhrawardy, was at New College. The Ali brothers were at Lincoln. Among others were A.R. Siddiqi and Shoaib Qureshi. The connection is puzzling because Aligarh's European Principals were all Cambridge men, as were almost all the European staff. It may be, when the tempestuous history of Aligarh is considered, that the preference for Oxford was a reaction against Cambridge teachers; or perhaps the attraction of Oxford was due to the reputation of the immensely learned D.S. Margoliouth, Professor of Arabic.[54]

One of the periods which is best documented is that immediately after the First World War. S.W.R.D. Bandaranaike, subsequently Prime Minister of Ceylon, who was at Christ Church from 1919 to 1923, has left some eighty pages of reminiscences on the experiences of himself and of the Indian students at Oxford.

His initial impression was of deep depression in a damp, grey, sunless winter, in a college of cliques and sets, in which Englishmen with whom he thought he had made friends would ignore him next day. He decided that 'before I am their equal, I must become their superior, because the attitude of racial superiority makes it easier to win respect than friendship'. Success in the Oxford Union eventually made him lasting friends.

As a Ceylonese, his viewpoint is unusually interesting. He regretted that the Indians had created an Indian Oxford within Oxford, the fault being not solely with either side, but having its roots in the differing psychology of the two nations. In general he concluded that the disadvantages outbalanced the advantages of an Oxford education for Indians, except for the ICS. A few Indians, he considered, should be selected by a committee, rather along the lines of the Rhodes Scholarships, for intellectual ability and aptitude for games. The rest should be encouraged to study at home, and then be given two years' supervised travel in Britain, USA, and France.[55] Bandaranaike himself read Classical Moderations and Law, and from his reminiscences it may not

be fanciful to hear, when he became Prime Minister, as leader of a
socialist or populist party, some echo of Oxford behind his praise of
the Commonwealth for its features of a democratic parliamentary form
of government, an independent judiciary, and an administration free
from undue political influence.

This post-war era coincided with the Amritsar massacre, Gandhi's
first civil disobedience campaign, and the Khilafat movement, all of
which imposed unusual strains on students torn between nationalism
and the desire to obtain qualifications, whether inside or outside the
ICS, which would support them in life. From the memoirs of K.P.S.
Menon, M.C. Chagla, N.B. Bonarjee, and others it seems a less happy
period than those earlier and later.[56] Menon, who obtained a First in
history and topped the ICS entry list, nevertheless considered that
Indian students suffered from a complex, resulting from the unnatural
relationship between the ruler and the ruled.

The number of Indians in residence was now considerable. L.R. Farnell
recounts that, when he was Vice-Chancellor in 1921, he received a
letter from Curzon, who at the time was both Foreign Secretary and
Chancellor of the University, expressing concern at the disloyalty
among Indian students. The Vice-Chancellor responded by summoning
all Indian students to meet him in the hall of Exeter College. The
meeting was abortive, as the hall was set on fire. At an adjourned
meeting, with suitable precautions, Farnell describes how 'he looked
down on 400 eyes gleaming from brown faces like panthers', and stated
categorically that 'anyone who comes here to sow discord and cause
disruption is a traitor to our academic fellowship: we must here preserve
the peace of God'.[57]

From memoirs of the 1930s the atmosphere seems happier. J.D.
Shukla, for example, who was at Corpus in the late 1930s, writes

It was so pleasant to be in Oxford. The wind of socialism blew
strong. It speaks a lot for the British tradition of freedom, and their
confidence in the openness of their society that they exposed us, the
civil servants of an empire, to the free and academic atmosphere of a
great university rather than a government institution.[58]

H.C. Gupta, who was at New College about the same time, recalls that
he was at first lonely and obliged to associate with other foreigners,
until (like many other Indians) he fell under the spell of the Oxford
Union, 'the eminently fair hearing accorded to contestants, and the
rapier thrusts of arguments and debate'.[59] In 1935 D.F. Karaka became

the first Indian to be President of the Union.

Indira Gandhi spent less than eighteen months at Somerville. She does not seem to have been much interested in her studies and was diverted by political interests, such as the Spanish War, and by a fiancé at the London School of Economics. In any case, she had to be removed to Switzerland for medical treatment.

Sadly, the records of the Indian Majlis cannot be traced. The society was founded by Mohammed Ali and others about 1908, and between then and the Partition of India in 1947 most Indian and Ceylonese students belonged to it. To keep a fair communal balance its proceedings began with the Bande Mataram and concluded with a hymn of Iqbal.

Indians coming to teach in Oxford only really made an impact after Independence, since when Indian, Pakistani, and Bangladeshi historians and economists have made notable contributions. From the memoirs of the ICS probationers, it would seem that the collaboration of Indian historians, economists, and language teachers might have considerably improved the courses.

The great exception before Independence was Radhakrishnan, who held the Spalding Chair of Eastern Religion from 1936 to 1952 at All Souls. He was an impressive lecturer, always wearing a turban, who could rise to heights of eloquence as when, during one of the civil disobedience campaigns, he gave an address on a text from the prophet Ezekiel. 'I will overturn, overturn, overturn it and it shall be no more until he come whose right it is, and I will give it to him.'[60]

Politics and courtesies apart however, though the university was proud to have such a distinguished and exotic scholar, it was not quite clear that there was always a meeting of minds between Radhakrishnan and Oxford's Greek and Latin philosophers.

Conclusions

This attempt to identify some themes of the relationship between Oxford and India, and to note their interconnection, leads us to recognize how much more research is required. It would be interesting to compare Oxford's approach and style with that of Cambridge in the promotion of Indian studies; in the influence on Indians and British administrators who studied there; and in the mission and educational field. To take two notable examples: Jawaharlal Nehru's ideas on economic and social planning were surely influenced by the fact that he studied natural sciences at Cambridge, rather than history or classics at Oxford; and Gandhi's most trusted British friend, C.F. Andrews, was a former Cambridge missionary, whom it is difficult to envisage as emerging from an Oxford Mission context. Why indeed did the Cambridge Mission in Delhi have such a different and more intellectual history than the Oxford Mission to Calcutta?

More examination is needed generally of Oxford's influence on imperial policies and racial attitudes in the crucial second half of the nineteenth century. In this, much attention to Balliol's record is indicated; for, although Christ Church furnished many Governors-General in the earlier part of the century, a number of these were aristocratic Etonians for whom Oxford was hardly more than a finishing school. At the end of the century, however, three successive Viceroys came from Balliol, heavily marked with Jowett's stamp. The degree of Balliol's involvement in India can be illustrated by the fact that, in 1914, 249 of its living graduates had served in the ICS. This was over 10 per cent of the total number of Balliol graduates alive and twice as many as those in the home civil service.[61]

A provisional reckoning may suggest that on the positive side Oxford's racial attitudes were civilized by the standards of their time; that the Oxford movement, though sometimes quaint, generally restrained Oxford from more strident and patriotic forms of evangelicalism; that the nature of the university's classical studies inculcated a strong sense of duty; and that this sense of duty caused Oxford's most influential teachers to oppose the more heartless policies of *laissez-faire*.

On the negative side, Nirad Chaudhuri has described the cult of Oxford among Indians as 'meretricious and even dubious'[62] and has attributed to Oxford a responsibility for the 'self-conscious and intellectually shoddy imperial sentiment of the late nineteenth century'. American observers (see, for example, R. Braibanti's *Administration and Economic Development in India* (1963), p. 9) have criticized the 'omnicompetent generalists', whom Oxford sent out as administrators, for their lack of understanding of the applied natural sciences – the Imperial School of Forestry, Oxford's main contribution in this field, was only established in the twentieth century. But the saddest failure was of the high hopes for making Oxford a great centre of Indian studies. The story of the Indian Institute deserves the attention of contemporary institutions for regional studies, both inside and outside Oxford, if we agree with Santayana that those who do not study their own history are doomed to repeat it.

Notes

1. Hamayun Kabir, *Britain and India* (New Delhi, 1960), p. 20ff.
2. *Dictionary of National Biography* – Boden, Joseph.
3. Monier Williams Papers, in possession of his family. Copies of some are in the Indian Institute, Oxford.
4. F. Max Mueller, *Life and Letters* (London, 1902), vol. I, p. 357.
5. Ibid., vol. II, p. 369.
6. Monier Williams Papers.
7. Max Mueller, *Life and Letters*, vol. II, p. 369.
8. *Record of Establishment of Indian Institute* (anon. n.d.) p. 48.
9. Ibid., p. 71.
10. Oxford University Archives, LL/M/1/13, Minutes of Curators of Indian Institute (1909).
11. See Debates and Flyleaves, *Oxford University Gazette* (June and July 1965).
12. R. Gombrich, 'On Being Sanskritic', Inaugural lecture (Oxford, 1978).
13. W.W. Hunter, 'A Forgotten Oxford Movement', *Fortnightly Review* (1896), p. 689.
14. Oxford University Archives, NW/16/1 and NW/16/6.
15. Bishop Heber in *Lives of Missionaries* (SPCK, London, n.d.), p. 169.
16. Ibid., p. 238.
17. J. Bateman, *Life of Rt. Rev. Daniel Wilson* (London, 1860); and J. Birks, *Life and Correspondence of T.V. French* (London, 1895).
18. G. Longridge, *History of Oxford Mission to Calcutta* (London, 1910), p. 137.
19. Fr O'Neill, 'Brahmoism, is it for us or against us', Pusey House Collection, and E.G. Willis, Letter to Regius Professor of Pastoral Theology (Oxford, 1879).
20. Longridge, *History*, pp. 88 and 28.
21. Ibid., p. xiii.
22. *Father Douglass of Behala* by Some of his Friends (London, 1952), and Sister Gertrude, *Mother Edith* (London, 1964).
23. R.M. Benson, *Letters* (London, 1916), p. 63.
24. *Fr Douglass of Behala*, p. 150.
25. B. Spangenberg, *British Bureaucracy in India* (New Delhi, 1976), p. 18f.
26. R. Symonds, *The British and their Successors* (London, 1966), p. 25f.
27. Ibid., p. 34.
28. R.J. Moore, *Sir Charles Wood's Indian Policy* (Manchester, 1966), p. 89.
29. E. Abbott and L. Campbell, *Life and Letters of B. Jowett* (New York, 1897), p. 348.
30. Ibid., p. 119.
31. *Oxford Magazine* (24 February 1892).
32. 'District Officers Collection' in the India Office Library, London (material compiled by R.C.C. Hunt and J. Harrison for 'The District Officer', London, 1981).
33. R.M. Ogilvie, *Latin and Greek* (London, 1964).
34. Ibid., p. 117.
35. N. Mitchell, *Sir Geo. Cunningham* (London, 1968), p. 171.
36. S.W.R.D. Bandaranaike, *Speeches and Writings* (Colombo, 1963), p. 19.
37. Abbott and Campbell, *Life and Letters*, p. 122.
38. M. O'Dwyer, *India as I knew it* (London, 1925), p. 19.
39. Monier Williams Papers.
40. Coupland Papers, Box 5, Rhodes House, Oxford.
41. Oral communication from H.G. Alexander, who was present.
42. Abbott and Campbell, *Life and Letters*, p. 126.

43. Thomas Arnold, *Introductory Lectures on Modern History* (London, 1842), pp. 1–43.

44. W.D. Arnold, *Oakfield* (London, 1854), p. 118 and *passim*. Also F. Woodward, *The Doctor's Disciples* (London, 1954), p. 180f.

45. Sidney J. Owen, *India on the Eve of the British Conquest* (London, 1872), p. 20ff. In fairness, it may be noted that the Reader's duties under the University Statutes were to lecture on 'the Rise, Growth, and Organization of the British Power in India'.

46. A.L. Basham in C.H. Philips (ed.), *Historians of India and Pakistan* (London, 1962), p. 272.

47. Sir Verney Lovett, *History of the Indian Nationalist Movement* (London, 1920), p. 157.

48. P.E. Roberts, 'Review of V. Smith's *History of India*', *Oxford Magazine* (1919–20), p. 18.

49. Oxford University Archives, I/I/6.

50. Sir Herbert Risley in *Man*, vol. X (1910), p. 163.

51. V. Elwin, *The Tribal World of Verrier Elwin* (OUP Bombay, 1964).

52. J. Foster *Oxford Men and their Colleges* (Oxford, 1893); and *Alumni Oxoniensis Oxford* (Oxford, 1888).

53. Cornelia Sorabji, *India Calling* (London, 1934).

54. Deborah Lavin suggests that Lionel Curtis, who visited Aligarh, may have been responsible for the Oxford connection.

55. Bandaranaike, *Speeches and Writings*, pp. 12–75.

56. K.P.S. Menon, *Many Worlds* (1965); M.C. Chagla, *Roses in December* (Bombay, 1974); N.B. Bonarjee, *Under Two Masters* (London, 1970).

57. L.R. Farnell, *An Oxonian Looks Back* (London, 1934), p. 298.

58. 'District Officers Collection', India Office Library, 'J.D. Shukla' and 'H.C. Gupta'.

59. Ibid.

60. K.I. Dutt, *S. Radhakrishnan* (New Delhi, 1966), p. 20.

61. *Balliol College Register* (Oxford, 1914), p. vii.

62. N.C. Chaudhuri, *Scholar Extraordinary* (London, 1974), p. 205.

Part Two

SPECIAL CASES

4 CECIL RHODES AND THE SOUTH AFRICAN CONNECTION: 'A GREAT IMPERIAL UNIVERSITY'?

Colin Newbury

In his declining years Rhodes thought of Africa as 'the most dangerous portion of the Empire'.[1] With the folly of the Jameson Raid behind him and evidence of the protracted bitterness between Boer and Briton on every hand, he had good reason to indulge the self-doubts and fears of failure that had been the lot of proconsuls and politicians in the graveyard of imperial good intentions. For, by 1901, with his final Will and its codicils already signed, Rhodes had ceased to make his mark on the rapidly changing economic and political landscape in the southern region of the continent and was ready to leave the crucible in which he had won a fortune and damaged a reputation.

Yet he remained such a name for historians to conjure with that any account of the origins of his bequest entails a discussion of the ways in which his money was made, as well as the circumstances connecting that bequest with Oxford. Anyone, therefore, who takes up Rhodes and the Trust as his theme will find the path to the imperial 'north' so well blazed by Rhodes's biographers and several thousands of Rhodes Scholars that he might expect to find answers to his enquiry in the conventional route map of the empire-builder who pioneered the connection.

The trail leads, as is well known, across Natal and Griqualand West in the 1870s with occasional excursions to England and Oxford where a pass degree was taken at the end of 1881. Thereafter, the pioneer was firmly committed to the industrial, agricultural, and political expansion of British South Africa through minerals, land settlement, and manipulation of the more recalcitrant 'factors' — Imperial, Afrikaner, Ndebele, and Portuguese — from his headquarters in the Cape Cabinet and the board rooms of powerful companies. By the early 1890s Rhodes was famous — so much so that on one of his many treks to the imperial metropolis an honorary Doctorate of Civil Law was offered by his old university in 1892, but was deferred while 'the great amalgamator' (as he was styled in the chauvinist press)[2] removed obstacles in his path. Lobengula was crushed, but Kruger was not. The failure of the Raid wrecked the political base constructed at the Cape with consummate skill. The economic base at Kimberley and on the Rand was more than sufficient, however, to bear the cost of this disaster and help finance Rhodes's chartered British South Africa Company to exploit its major asset — land — while British South Africa and the empire drifted into war with an alienated Transvaal. A few months before that struggle began, the discredited but still influential amalgamator took up the offer of the Doctorate of Civil Law *honoris causa* which was conferred at Oxford in July 1899 amid a certain amount of dissent. He also laid down the main lines of his last munificent Will for an educational trust that year, thus refining a scheme which has its origins, like his degree, in the early 1890s. With immortality certain Rhodes returned to South Africa to make it safer for the empire by settling Britons in the annexed republics.

A career with such monuments along the way was certain to inspire overstatement about motivation and character, if charted mainly with Rhodes in mind. Understandably Rhodes's death in March 1902 promoted this cult of imperial personality by releasing a flood of eulogy, as the empire paid homage to one of its heroes. The publicity given to the Will of 1899, particularly the annotated version brought out by W.T. Stead, did much to reinstate the expansionist businessman and politician as a generous idealist.[3] By accepting this edited account of the vision behind the bequest of close on four million pounds, it was possible to reconcile Rhodes the mystic and developer of Central Africa with Rhodes the manipulator and promoter of the Raid. Stead's theory of a split personality became a good peg on which to hang a biography. And this approach, at least, was some improvement on the early hagiography turned out by his secretaries, Le Sueur and Jourdan, or by his banker and trustee, Sir Lewis Michell.[4] It squared, too, with some of the evidence collected later by Basil Williams about Rhodes's 'curiously duplex nature'.[5] In any case England needed a magnanimous hero in the last months before the Treaty of Vereeniging. Financiers, adventurers, charlatans, it was agreed, had plotted and profited during the struggle for British hegemony in southern Africa, but Stead's 'real Rhodes dwelt apart in the sanctuaries of his imagination'.[6]

This 'strong, silent' image does not really help anyone trying to trace the shifts in Rhodes's thinking about the employment of his wealth. Stead was not a very reliable guide. As editor of the *Pall Mall Gazette* and the *Review of Reviews* he was a quixotic partisan of imperial federation and an early colleague of Milner. His friendship with Rhodes, the rising colonial magnate who assisted the *Gazette* with £20,000 on his way up, was founded more on mutual admiration than on knowledge of the environment in which Rhodes worked. In a sense the great manipulator nearly became the manipulated, when Stead sought to further his own ideas on southern Africa through Rhodes and the Princess Radziwill, until a breach occurred in 1901 over Milner's policies and the future status of the Afrikaner republics.[7] Not even Stead's own biographer in two volumes can remove the impression that his subject had only a sketchy appreciation of the South African end of Rhodes's career at Kimberley, the Cape, or Central Africa in the 1890s.[8] Instead of a detailed memoir in the edition of *The Last Will*, we are left with half-formulated ideas and scraps of imperial intuition to explain the life and thought of the great man.

Basil Williams was much better placed by his access to contemporary sources and wrote a well-balanced book which has remained a standard work since 1921.[9] The conclusions are not particularly flattering to Rhodes's image, but the focus is still on the hero as a historical force in comparison with Clive, Caesar, or Napoleon, the imperial leader whose 'star suddenly failed him at a crucial moment'.[10] One of Williams's informants, John X. Merriman, warned against this idealization, but excused Rhodes as 'a sort of colonial Walpole' who fell victim to the stockjobbers.[11] The temptation to explain away was irresistable, and the earliest detractors such as F.J. Dormer and later ones like William Plomer and Felix Gross turn their explanations on unique and fatal flaws in their imperial Lucifer.[12] Even the most authoritative of the biographies by Lockhart and Woodhouse is not free from this Schumpeterian conception of the innovating personality, acting for good or ill on the raw material of human society, implicit in their subtitle: *The Colossus of Southern Africa.*[13]

It is, of course, the proper business of biographers to explore the personalities of their subjects. But Rhodes's written sources are not suitable for an analysis of how his mind worked at private levels. There are no diaries, but plenty of telegrams and speeches. More is written to Rhodes than by him, and some of the correspondence on business affairs is enigmatic in its raw state.

Secondly, the historiography of southern Africa is such a rapidly developing field that its personalities may for a time be dwarfed by accounts of the enormous structural changes in capitalist enterprise in the last third of the nineteenth century. At least one biographer has recognized this shift in emphasis towards a better understanding of the background of investment on the Rand or the origins of the British South Africa Company and has taken new material into account in his summary of Rhodes's manoeuvres and the limitation on his range of options.[14]

Finally, the older portrait of Rhodes as a pure politician above the intricate dealings of brokers and promoters is due for drastic revision, as the sources for his ventures into mining are exploited. It is already clear that he flourished during the diamond and gold rushes by learning important lessons in company management and the adaptation of legislation and regulations to the cause of business enterprise.[15] The precise relationship between the financial and engineering technicians of Kimberley and the Rand, on the one hand, and the colonial and imperial politicians who supported or opposed them, on the other, will doubtless be the theme of further works following the lead given by Cartwright, Blainey, Jeeves, Kubicek, and others who have used the signpost set up long ago by J.A. Hobson in 1900 and the more sophisticated directions of Herbert S. Frankel. The point is that new material on the history of the companies directed by Rhodes will entail some reassessment of the man himself, as the complex evolution of capitalization and production techniques in the regional economy is better understood. For it was out of the 'diamond pits', as Rhodes once claimed, that capital was accumulated first to finance the audacious manoeuvres leading to conflict with the agrarian and pastoral societies of the region.[16]

While the foregoing may seem obvious enough in the context of southern African historiography, it is still not clear just how the Will in its final form was to be funded by the product of Rhodes's business career, and still less the precise reasons for Rhodes's patronage of his old university. These two questions will occupy the bulk of this paper.

In the many biographies the connection between Rhodes, the undistinguished student, and Rhodes, the benefactor, seems to be assumed rather than demonstrated. All the biographers have difficulty with the decade of the 1870s which is tricked out with anecdotes (collected years later) and the oft-cited nonsense about the 'secret society' to be devoted to Anglo-Saxon hegemony and the recovery of the United States which appears in the earliest of the Wills and is continued in the crude race patriotism of the 'Confession of Faith' written at Oxford in June 1877.[17] Sir Lewis Michell, therefore, assumed that imperial questions which may have interested Oxford students in the 1870s were of interest to Rhodes and a stimulus to his later schemes for expansion in South Africa and British leadership in the world at large: 'and one can picture the young Kimberley digger, with his great Will in his pocket, and his head full of high schemes for the expansion of the race which he believed to be the finest in the world'.[18]

But, if this is so, Rhodes disguised his enthusiasm fairly success-fully and avoided all the usual undergraduate circles for airing contem-porary political questions. He was never a member of the Union and never attended any of its meetings on the Eastern Question or the impending ruin of the empire by the Liberals. He almost certainly never met Milner or Asquith who were up in 1876-7 and were already keenly interested in such topics. Nor did he attend the one relevant Union debate in May 1878, when he was still in residence, on the desirability of imperial federation (a motion lost by fifteen votes to eleven).[19] Even John Flint, whose chapter on 'Diamonds and Oxford' is the most sensible account of Rhodes's life at this period, follows Lockhart and Woodhouse by taking it for granted that Rhodes was left with a lasting appreciation of the university's 'mystic mantel of greatness'.[20] For-tunately he stops short, where the older biographies do not, in attributing influence to Ruskin's lectures on the 'new gospel of beauty and public service'.[21] For there is no evidence that Rhodes ever heard or read any of this romantic exhortation, condemned even by Milner as 'the drivel of the idiot Ruskin'.[22] And it seems highly unlikely that 'the young Kimberley digger' who had already learned to manage African labour would have succumbed to Ruskin's effort to inculcate the virtues of unselfish toil through voluntary work by dons and undergraduates on a half-finished road at Hinksey.[23]

One is driven to the conclusion, therefore, that all attempts to make plausible connections between Rhodes the undergraduate dipping into a mixture of classics, literature, and law, and his subsequent patronage of the university are tenuous in the extreme. And to some extent this view is confirmed by the inability of Basil Williams's Oxford informants to remember anything much about a student who lived in digs and was never in residence at Oriel, and by Rochfort Maguire's testimony that Rhodes was only interested in the Drag and the Masonic lodge as his extra-curricular activities.[24]

A more likely proposition is that Oxford was not really essential to his later ideas on empire and the place of South African territories in a confederal or unitary scheme; and that the scholarship plan, and therefore the educational trust in the Will, had its origins also outside the university so closely associated with Rhodes's name. In retrospect, perhaps, the collegiate element essential to Oxford's system of instruc-tion appealed more to Rhodes as benefactor of American and colonial men from heterogeneous backgrounds than it had to Rhodes the undergraduate himself.

It would seems probable that an explanation for Rhodes's imperial sentiments should be sought first in the colonial environment where he worked. For someone who had pioneered in Natal in the early 1870s and whose brother, Herbert Rhodes, was friend and companion to Frederic Elton, adviser to Shepstone, an awareness of colonial expansiveness and the perennial problems of land, labour, and capital in conditions of poor infrastructure was as ordinary as discussion of crop prices and the weather.[25] An examination of Natal newspapers for the period shows that Carnarvon's federation scheme and the sub-imperial ambitions of local colonists provided material for more lively debate than the Oxford Union.

By moving to Griqualand West, moreover, Rhodes acquired first-hand experience of the legal and institutional benefits of annexation, at the expense of the Cape's rival and neighbour the Orange Free State. One should remember that Rhodes's early interest in Oxford was largely vocational, in the sense that he thought a law degree would help him make his way on the diamond fields; and it is known that he contemplated reading for the Bar, until he was caught up in the intensive and instructive course in mining development that filled the years when he was not away at Oxford. Even so, it was not certain he would remain in South Africa before 1880, when De Beers Mining Company was founded. His decision to remain was undoubtedly influenced by his third source of experience in the benefits of the imperial connection, namely his entry into the Cape legislature in 1881 as one of the two Members for Barkly West.

If this emphasis on his colonial experience is allowed in the formation of his views of metropolitan assistance for a largely autonomous settler society, then Rhodes's aim of imperial expansion and control was African, and not London, centred. This was completely consistent with the derivation of the wealth required to finance expansion. But just how Rhodes made his money, or how much he was worth, is a story which biographers leave obscure for lack of the necessary business histories of all the enterprises in which he invested. From the *prima facie* evidence of his estate as inherited by his trustees and some lists of his assets in the 1890s, one would conclude that the basis of Rhodes's wealth remained, as it had begun, with diamond mining.[26] This conclusion is somewhat at variance with the considerable emphasis that has been placed on founder shareholdings in the United Concessions Company which grew out of Central Search in 1890.[27] These were certainly a source of speculative profit, when shares acquired a premium value, but Rhodes's final holding of British South Africa Company shares (some 19,333) represented about 2 per cent of his estate at current values, and this was soon reduced to insignificant proportions.[28] Rhodes's wealth, therefore, owed something in the short term to 'Kaffir circuses' on the Rand, but much more to monopoly production by amalgamation at Kimberley. A survey of his business papers suggests it owed little to settlement in Mashonaland or the plunder of the Ndebele in 1893, whatever the later development of the territory to which Rhodes gave his name. It is from his earliest business experience that his capital accumulation derives. And it is from this accumulation that the Trust was funded.

For the restructuring of De Beers Consolidated in 1888 and 1889 created a production monopoly for nearly two decades which was coupled with a marketing monopoly through the operation of a diamond syndicate of leading merchants. Rhodes found himself as a leading participant in a group system with interests in the Rand and to a lesser extent in his chartered enterprise. As Chairman of De Beers he was in a position to utilize the most extraordinary articles of association (or trust deed) authorizing any series of investments or acquisitions his board could be persuaded to agree to and which the shareholders would tolerate. Moreover, along with three other directors, Rhodes was a life governor with the bulk of the founder shares and special participation in profit distribution.

He proceeded immediately to employ company assets to build up a reserve fund in the City as collateral for raising loans to finance his Mashonaland and associated schemes. With the help of a small number of the London directors of the board he shipped out diamonds secretly from the Cape and had them sold outside the syndicate for British consols.[29] Production returns for De Beers mines were falsified to put the diamond merchants off the scent.[30] When the scheme was discovered in 1892, the chairman of the London section of the board, Philipson Stow, was blamed and he resigned his chairmanship and sold out his life governorship emoluments to Alfred Beit, one of the three life governors, and Rhodes, finally resigning from the company in 1898. The policy of building up reserves and investing in mines and land was continued, however, as sound business practice, though there was disagreement among the directors as to how far Rhodes's particular schemes would be approved by shareholders. But he secured investment of £100,000 in his chartered company in 1894 and was able to borrow some £330,000 against the diamond reserve, before the events of the Raid lessened confidence in his judgement and the board made its decisions on more orthodox lines.

Nevertheless Rhodes's personal wealth benefited enormously from the conservative concentration of the bulk of the directors in Kimberley and London on production and marketing in the 1890s. There was a high rate of return on capital invested which was kept deliberately low, and from 1896 40 per cent dividends were paid every year prior to Rhodes's death, except 1900. Barnato's death in 1897 left his life governorship earnings to the two remaining founder directors, Beit and Rhodes. These two participated in the increased profits of the company, after a fixed percentage of dividends had been paid and after redemption of debentures and interest. On this latter point there was a protracted and acrimonious argument between Rhodes and the board throughout 1898 and 1899 which touched on his past policy of investing in South African and other development schemes for political as well as economic gain. When the life governors' share of profits mounted to over £150,000 per year, there was a direct conflict of interest between Beit and Rhodes on one side and the directors representing shareholders on the other.

From this dangerous impasse, which threatened to become public, Rhodes and Beit were rescued by an agreement to reconstruct De Beers capital by a split into deferred and preferred shares, 160,000 of which were voted to the two founders who surrendered their rights as life governors.

This reconstruction, which solved a number of internal problems in the direction of the company, also helps explain the dramatic change in the relative value of Rhodes's assets between the earliest listing we have in the 1890s and the list of company shares in the Will. At the period prior to the Raid Rhodes was worth about £1.5 millions, according to his own estimates. Diamond shares accounted for 40 per cent, while his gold fields and other Rand mining shares made up 33.7 per cent. By 1902 gold mining interests were much reduced compared with the massive value of De Beers stocks paid over in compensation for surrender of the life governorship and which appear in the first years of the Rhodes Trust accounts.

This fortunate commutation of the perpetual interest of the two life governors into shares also provides an insight into Rhodes's conception of a deed of trust to carry on his intentions for education, agricultural development, and political support for the English-speaking element in South Africa. Those intentions were clarified slowly in the course of his career and were influenced as much by the Anglo-Boer conflict which overshadowed his last years as by the means at his disposal to help heal the divisions resulting from that conflict. The 'idea' rather vaguely outlined in his 'Confession of faith' and the concept of a 'secret society' operating to spread British values were given a more positive form and a mechanism to control the necessary funding. The Trustees chosen by Rhodes were in no ordinary position of responsibility: Lord Rothschild, Stead, and the lawyer Hawksley, who were to manage his estate in the Will of 1892, were all closely associated with Rhodes's early company promotion and were expected to understand his views. The last Will of 1899 nominated Lord Rosebery and Lord Grey, Stead, Alfred Beit, Rhodes's banker Lewis Michell, and the indispensable Hawksley. Codicils replaced Stead by Milner and added Jameson as a Trustee. After the objectives of the Will had been financed, it was made clear they were residuary legatees of all real and personal estate. They were, in short, life governors of Rhodes's enterprises with a knowledge of his purposes, left conveniently vague outside the details of the scholarship.

Apart from Milner they were political friends and business partners from the period before the Raid. After the consolidation of De Beers and the granting of the British South Africa Company charter, Rhodes exerted his greatest metropolitan influence among the Liberals of Gladstone's fourth administration from late 1892. He promised to extend the railway from Bechuanaland Colony through the Protectorate and run the territory for £40,000, saving the government £100,000 annually; he offered to take over Uganda and run it as a province of the South Africa Company for £24,000 annually; a canal scheme was proposed to link 'Zambesia' to the great lakes; and he laid claim to a large part of the Congo basin.[31] In the Harcourt 'Diaries' there are glimpses of him moving in the highest circles and dining with the Ripons, the Kimberleys, the Chancellor of the Exchequer, and Randolph Churchill. Probably he hoped the Liberals would give the Cape and the chartered company a free hand to expand north; for Harcourt noted that 'even Jingoism is tolerable when it is done "on the cheap"'.[32] It also helped to subscribe £5,000 to depleted party funds. Before Rosebery fell from power, Rhodes was made Privy Councillor in February 1895; and in March he succeeded in the ultimate political jobbery of getting the ancient and compliant fellow-director of De Beers, Sir Hercules Robinson, to replace Loch as High Commissioner at the Cape.

This, too, is the period when he took it upon himself as Cape Prime Minister to confer with other colonial ministers on tariffs and lobbied Harcourt for a change in the Cobden Treaty to benefit Cape wine growers. He mildly admonished Sir Henry Parkes for using the term 'Commonwealth' instead of 'Dominion' for the projected federation of

Australia.[33] Above all, he sold himself as an honest broker between the Cape and the Transvaal, the man most likely to bring the recalcitrant neighbouring state safely into the imperial orbit by confederation.[34] If not at the height of his wealth, Rhodes was at the zenith of his political influence.

Subsequent events leading to his fall from this pinnacle do not concern this paper. But the early part of this period before 1895 saw the genesis of the scholarships. It is also the period when Rhodes moved into close association with Alfred Beit, after their purchase of Stow's life governorship emoluments in 1893, when they agreed to co-operate on future policy in De Beers and Rhodes's 'further plans and aspirations' in the north.[35] We do not know whether Beit was informed about the contents of Rhodes's Will of 1893 which first contained the provision for scholarships. But it was against this background of successful company promotion, financial intrigue, and the harmonious co-operation with metropolitan Liberals by a wealthy and adroit colonial politician that Oxford's South African connection was founded.

The origins of the idea of imperial scholarships lie quite simply in the patriotic cultural exchanges promoted by the editors of *Greater Britain* in 1891, as a substitute for an unlikely imperial federation. An Australian expatriate, Professor T. Hudson Beare, drew up a plan for 'Britannic Scholarships' which was published the following year as part of a series of articles on the celebration of a British 'Race Festival' (a distant forerunner of the Commonwealth Games).[36] Beare's article outlined in some detail a scheme for funding a hundred scholars at British universities from all the principal colonies. The Imperial Government was invited to provide £20,000 annually towards the cost which was to be refunded by each colony, and Beare also suggested post-graduate travelling scholarships to enable British students to undertake research work on resources and markets in the colonies, especially in India.

> On his return to his Colony each student would form a nucleus around which would gather all that was best, and each would form another of those invisible ties, stronger than any which can be devised by the cunning of law-makers, which will, we hope, keep together, for good or ill, the Anglo-Saxon race.[37]

There is fairly strong, but not conclusive, evidence that this idea was passed on to Rhodes, when he was in London late in 1892, according to J. Astley Cooper (one of the the editors of *Greater Britain*) and that

Sir Henry Loch who was also in town was kept informed.[38] Rhodes's Will of December 1892, completed in some haste before he left, shows for the first time an appreciation of 'the Oxford and Cambridge system' to be applied in his plan for local scholarships for South African College.[39] But it is unlikely that he contemplated financing anything as elaborate as the kind of scheme proposed by Cooper and Beare, given his heavy financial commitments to the chartered company and the cost of the Matabele War of 1893.

With that war out of the way, however, and with Consolidated Gold Fields of South Africa soundly based within a group system on the Rand, Rhodes's finances looked more buoyant, as speculation in Ndebele lands raised chartered shares and sales of De Beers diamonds recovered from the recession of 1890-2. In a new Will drawn up in 1893, it is arguable that he felt able to make provision for an imperial scholarship scheme of more modest scope than the Beare plan. There is a close resemblance between the reasons used to justify his funding for thirty-six scholars from South Africa, Australia, New Zealand, and Canada and those given by Beare; Oxford, rather than Edinburgh, was chosen because of its collegiate facilities; but the system of nomination was less centralized than Beare's plan and left a good deal to local selection techniques.

Such an explanation can, of course, only be regarded as tentative, but it should be evaluated in conjunction with Rhodes's honorary Doctorate of Civil Law in 1892. Just whose idea this was cannot be ascertained from the available records. The only solid evidence is a minute of the Hebdomadal Council which reads that on 14 November Standing Orders were suspended and a ballot was taken, when 'the following Hon. degrees of DCL were agreed to: Hon. Cecil J. Rhodes moved by Master of Pemb. & Sir Henry B. Loch moved by Princ. of St. Ed. Hall'.[40] The fact that there were no similar awards at this period is less surprising than the appearance of the Cape Governor and High Commissioner in the same motion. The sponsors of Rhodes and Loch were inspired either by a fine sense of imperial protocol, or by a malicious sense of humour. For both men were equally importunate in their lobbying over the Bechuanaland railway concession; and the morning after the Council singled them out for joint honours, they met with Ripon at the Colonial Office in 'a bear fight' over ultimate control of this strategic and commercial line, which left Loch without any satisfactory decision and drove Rhodes into 'a white passion'.[41]

Rhodes must have agreed to accept the award, but he had to return immediately to South Africa, where he was fully occupied with

Lobengula and the Transvaal. When he felt able to come to Oxford to receive the degree in 1899, the climate of academic opinion had been changed by the findings of the Parliamentary Committee on the Raid. Some ninety-two dons got up a flysheet to express their regret to the Vice-Chancellor, D.B. Monro, and included among their number the Master of Balliol (E. Caird), the Reader in Indian Law (Sir William Markby), the Reader in Indian History (S. Owen), A.V. Dicey, and H.A.L. Fisher, later to become a Trustee.[42] There was even one lone objector from Rhodes's old college. But, remembering that Monro was also Provost of Oriel and that the terms of the revised Will of 1899 included a bequest of £100,000 to the college, it is difficult to believe that its Fellows did not have wind of this largesse when Rhodes received his degree along with Elgin and Kitchener on 21 June 1899.[43]

By the end of the century, then, Rhodes's name had been firmly linked with Oxford by a delayed piece of academic patronage and by a generous provision designed to strengthen the union of English-speaking peoples. The educational administration of the original American and Colonial Scholarships has been so well described by C.K. Allen, Frank Aydelotte, and Lord Elton, from the Oxford point of view, that it is useful to recall that there were other important charges on the estate arising in the context of South African political and economic history. Indeed, the Trust itself has become so much part of the Oxford landscape on the old Wadham Garden site that it is surprising to find that until the late 1920s much of the business of husbanding the £3.9 millions left by the testator was carried out by old and busy men at Milner's house in London, at Hawksley's chambers, and by Jameson and Michell at Cape Town. Meetings of the Trustees were rare occasions. Important decisions were taken by two or three and simply referred to the others for their opinions. The position of the Trustees as residuary legatees safeguarded Rhodes's intentions, but this sympathetically personal administration also exposed the Trust to the depredations of death duties, as his nominees died off. Regularly constituted funds for the different purposes envisaged by Rhodes were not really set up till 1921, and Rhodes House was not completed till the late 1920s. Only then did the educational side of the Trust clearly predominate over other aspects of Rhodes's enterprises.

For at the outset it was not intended that the Scholarships should absorb most of the annual revenues of the estate. There were political and developmental charges to be funded. In the year before his death Rhodes arranged for Michell to draw on De Beers for sums up to

£250,000, guaranteed in part by the diamond company, by Wernher, Beit and Company, and by Rhodes himself, to help settle British yeomen on confiscated land in the Transvaal and Orange River Colony.[44] There were investments in Rhodes's Fruit Farms at the Cape and some 200,000 acres at Bulawayo and Inyanga to be serviced with subsidies; and there were important ranching and irrigation schemes begun by Abe Bailey and Sir T.W. Smartt, funded by De Beers and the Trust.

There was, furthermore, a special political fund known as the 'sub-trust' or the 'Rhodes-Beit Shares Fund' set up in 1907 with a revenue from 26,667 De Beers shares. The accounts for this fund for the period 1908-25 show that about £173,000 was expended in seventeen years.[45] The largest amount (£90,000) went directly to Cape and Transvaal politicians such as Sir Percy Fitzpatrick, who received £4,500 annually, T.W. Smartt, Lionel Phillips, and Sir Alfred Hennessy. There was a heavy outlay on the South African Association and the Progressive party during Cape and Transvaal elections in 1910. Amery drew on this source for some £5,000 between 1919 and 1920, and Lionel Curtis for a total of £7,255 in 1908. The *Round Table* was subsidized from it till 1915, and again in 1921; and Milner used some £5,000 for unspecified disbursements. There were minor payments to the British South Africa Company, the Royal Geographical Society, Jameson, Gardner Williams, former manager of De Beers, and other old associates. But most expenditure is concentrated in the pre-war years, though there are entries under the Cape Political Fund as late as 1925. All this, too, was very much within the terms of the Will and Rhodes's desire for the 'maintenance and extension of the Imperial thought by a party literature', as he had directed Hawksley in 1899.[46]

The major question which had to be faced by the Trustees, however, was whether the estate could stand these multifarious charges and keep the Scholarships going. Very wisely Beit and Michall had agreed with Grey and Milner to set aside deferred De Beers shares to produce an income 'of £125,000 from March 1903 which was more than sufficient to cover scholarship expenses (some £52,000) and make investments in South African agricultural schemes. They also began to move out of De Beers stocks into government securities of various kinds, a practice enthusiastically continued by Milner.

Their other principal achievement was the appointment of George Parkin whose tact and organizing skill removed the doubts of the dons and made it possible for Oxford to take the first Scholars in October 1903. But the great publicity given to the Will by Stead meant that the Trust was importuned with plans for tapping seemingly limitless funds for worthy causes. Schemes were quickly thought up for a military academy, for the reform of South African education, for training the South African civil service, and for propping up institutions such as the Diocesan College at Rondebosch. Copies of the Will printed by the Colonial Office were distributed to ten colonial governors at an Oxford conference in July 1902 which must have bemused them, as none of their territories, except Canada, were beneficiaries. Sir Alfred Jones offered free passages for Jamaican and Canadian Scholars using his shipping lines.

Amid all this enthusiasm, the dons encouraged by Parkin began to look for hand-outs, too, in order to build up the educational infrastructure. Was Oxford fit to receive Rhodes Scholars? Sir Edward Bagnall Poulton, staunch Darwinian and Hope Professor of Zoology, thought not and pleaded with Milner for a cool £1 million to expand the sciences. He thought to found 'a great Imperial University' (the subtitle of this chapter), while Parkin (from whom he borrowed this phrase) argued the cause of Oxford's modernization:

> If Rhodes had had some friend at his elbow who knew Oxford he would have advised him to give $\frac{5}{6}$ of his bequest to the fellows and $\frac{1}{6}$ to the University in order to give full effect to the fund. I feel sure that in some way £5,000 to £10,000 a year must be raised to put the place in a condition to do justice not merely to the newcomers but to its own present [system?] under conditions of modern life.[47]

But the Trustees could see no reason to settle more on Oxford, bearing in mind that the Will was not simply for educational purposes in England. They founded two chairs at Grahamstown instead. It was left to Alfred Beit shortly before his own death to write somewhat regally to the Vice-Chancellor in June 1904 expressing surprise that there was no provision for teaching the 'History of our Dominions over the Sea':

> As I am anxious to promote a greater interest in, and a more accurate knowledge of this particular branch of British history amongst the students of the University, more especially amongst those who under the provisions of Mr. Rhodes' Will come to Oxford from all parts of the Empire, I now request you to submit to the University authorities the following proposal, viz:—
> To contribute the sum of £1,310 per annum for 7 years (1) For the maintenance of a resident Professor of Colonial History — (2) For

Assistant Lecturers - (3) For a prize of £50 for an annual essay on the advantages of 'Imperial Citizenship' and for the payment of Examiners' fees — (4) For the purchase of books on the subject, the amount of such purchase not to exceed £50 per annum.[48]

A permanent endowment was promised and other conditions were laid down. Beit lived just long enough to approve the selection of H.E. Egerton as the first incumbent, made at a meeting in the Colonial Office at the end of 1905.

The truth was that there was little enough to spare from income in the Trust to invest in Oxford. Between 1904 and 1907, when the Trustees bought a variety of government stocks by selling off 90,000 De Beers shares, diamond prices were on the decline and slumped badly during the American recession at the end of that period. The value of the original estate fell slightly. About half of the income had been invested in consolidated stocks and the other half in South African fruit and dams. The scholarship trust was well covered, but there was a constant drain of fixed charges to support the Bulawayo and Inyanga estates and some doubtful investments in Rhodes's Farms (£95,401), and the Smartt Syndicate which ate up no less than £200,000 between 1907 and 1909, of which half had been put up by the Trust and paid no dividend. By 1914 the list of Trust investments was valued at £3.4 millions of which about one-third was still in De Beers, one-third in British, American, Colonial, and Latin American fixed interest securities, plus a lot of doubtful odds and ends in Mashonaland Railways, Rhodesia Railways, and the affairs of Dr Smartt.

Moreover, opinions were divided between Michell and Milner over the most desirable emphasis within the terms of the Will. Michell complained that the Trustees and the public concentrated too much on education instead of more investment in South African mining and agriculture to escape the perils of 'revolutionary socialism' in England.[49] Milner, on the other hand, persisted in his predeliction for American investment and got his fingers badly burned in an Idaho irrigation company which cost the Trust $50,000.

There was a much more serious crisis by 1915, when diamond dividends were suspended and the Trust's stock had to be written down by 20 per cent. For the first time there was a deficit on the income and expenditure account, and the scholarship fund was only kept going because there were no German Scholars and fewer Americans and colonials in residence. Milner's reluctance to go to parliament to ask for powers to redistribute the German Scholarships further exacerbated relations with Michell, though the Rhodes Estate bill of 1916 was passed without any trouble. Michell resisted redistribution to the Transvaal (which was given one of the five available Scholarships) on the grounds that young Stellenbosch students might become as disloyal as the Germans and that Rhodes had not made his money there but at Kimberley.[50] He succeeded, however, in getting Milner to agree to a thorough audit of the Trust's accounts, and he trimmed off some of the South African largesse such as payments to the City Club at Cape Town, the Umtali Club, and the perpetual debts of Diocesan College. Michell also raised the point, first brought up by Parkin, that, because of the poor health of the remaining Trustees, the scholarship fund should be transferred 'to the authorities at Oxford' with a large enough capital grant to provide for increased expenditure.[51] South Africa, where Botha had a 'rebel vote in the Transvaal and the Orange Free State', now looked a more dangerous outlet for investment than England at war.

Milner and Rosebery approved the idea of adding new Trustees, but Milner firmly opposed handing anything over to Oxford:

> I am quite sure that we could not render greater dis-service to Oxford itself than by giving up our independent position as regards the scholarships. The last thing we want to happen is to have them run by Dons with donnish ideas. The Rhodes Trust has done valuable service to Oxford by letting in a fresh stream of influence into the University. No body of typically Oxford Dons could possibly have done what Parkin has, just because, though he himself had been at Oxford and was in thorough sympathy with her, he yet remained in a sense an outsider and a Canadian. Nothing is more needed than an interpreter, a bridge so to speak, between academic Oxford and the 'young barbarians' whose introduction into academic Oxford has been of such enormous advantage to her. The thing will never work as it ought to work, or produce the effect which Rhodes intended it to produce, if you get a lot of crusted old Dons at Oxford to run it. There are a few men, like A.L. Smith of Balliol, who have the width of sympathy and the youthfulness of spirit which would qualify them, but they are, believe me, the rare exceptions, and probably would be the first to deprecate anything like the handing over of the management of the scholarship trust to the University.[52]

But clearly the Trust itself could not escape the financial consequences of the war and poor investments in South African agriculture.

Michell clung to the fruit farms and the Ongers River Estates, on the grounds that Rhodes had made the initial experiments in land settlement 'partly from political motives' and to build up a great fruit industry. But no dividend had been paid for fourteen years, and earnings had been ploughed back into cold storage, reclamation, vineyards, and a canning factory. The Trust still had one-third of the capital in the farms valued at £318,000 in 1916, but they had become a liability.

Temporarily the Trust's annual expenditure was saved by good returns from shares in City Deep Mines in 1915 and 1916, as much as by the virtual suspension of the Scholarships for the last two years of the war. South Africa and Canada were given four of the German Scholarships, and Wylie, the Trust's agent at Oxford, suggested using the spare one for the West Indies with some reservations: 'No doubt we must expect an occasional "coloured man" from Barbados or Trinidad, as we already do from Jamaica: but that can't be helped.'[53] Milner also favoured using the spare Scholarship for the neglected parts of the empire without committing himself to any particular territory, though he resisted the suggestion by Austen Chamberlain at the India Office to allocate all the German Scholarships to Indians, on the grounds that the statutory power to reallocate requested from parliament should not specify regions or countries.[54]

The major reorganization required came after 1917. Of the original Trustees two were dead; two had retired; Grey was constantly ill. Otto Beit, Jameson, and Milner were alive and reinforced by Lord Lovatt and Rudyard Kipling. In July 1917, after Otto Beit had reviewed all investments, a new scholarship fund was financed from War Loan stock, De Beers shares, Cape Government stock, and Rhodesia and Mashonaland Railway stock to yield an income of £85,000 annually. The crippling burden of death duties amounted to £158,000 lost by the passing of Beit, Grey, Hawksley, and Jameson as residuary legatees. This prompted a transfer of securities to a charitable trust fund and a general purposes fund and tied up about £1.7 millions by 1921 and partly got round the problem of retaining control through Trustees sympathetic to Rhodes's aims without giving the Inland Revenue a large share of the estate passed on to the surviving members of the Trust.

The restructuring also enabled the Trust to make a number of grants towards Oxford posts in Forestry, Criminal Law, Pathology, and Pharmacology, and for the Rhodes Chair in Imperial History in London. Lesser bequests from the general purposes fund included a monument to Jameson, sums to the Memorial Settlers' Association, and pittances

for Boy Emigration to Australia and the settlement of British Women
in Rhodesia. But on the whole there was a shift away from the political
purposes of the Trust to the cause of education in its various forms.
The last interest taken in Rhodes's Fruit Farms was a visit by Milner
in 1925 which produced pessimistic reports on poor management,
and some interesting suggestions by Lady Milner on the design of a
suitable label with the head of Rhodes to promote the sale of jams.

Wisely the Trust invested in Oxford instead in 1924, when the Beit
and Harmsworth collection became too much for the Bodleian. In
order to provide a library of official publications and 'for the first time
make a complete collection of official records and documents from all
parts of the empire', the Trustees resolved to build Rhodes House.[55]

The conclusion is, therefore, that the linkage between Rhodes and
Oxford resulted much less from the student days of a rather undistinguished undergraduate than from the importance of South Africa
to the imperial metropolis in the 1890s. Rhodes was first and foremost
a colonial politician with a talent for making capital work in under-
developed areas. He came to prominence as imperial trading and banking
facilities expanded and the empire began to go on the defensive against
competition from France and Germany. After the Baring crisis of
1890 and the collapse of three South African banks, the Cape Prime
Minister who kept the diamond market stable, invested in the supply
of gold, and who appeared to manage the Cape Afrikaners and
promised to settle the problem of the Transvaal looked like a safe
anchor-man in the most volatile of political economies. He was not
completely trusted – less perhaps by Conservatives than by the Liberals;
and there was an effort on the part of his friends and business colleagues
such as Albert Grey to make him respectable.[56] And it is probably
against that background of undoubted wealth and useful power at the Cape
that the award of the honorary Doctorate of Civil Law is to be viewed.

In return Rhodes was able to indulge his penchant for intrigue and
some of his fantasies and was encouraged to overreach himself in his
sub-imperial expansion northward. The fantasies included some poorly-
formulated notions at the level of race patriotism, which were given
substance when he encountered the more considered scholarship
proposals of Beare and the imperial enthusiasts who centred on *Greater
Britain* and Stead's *Pall Mall Gazette*. And they included his subversion
of Kruger's republic, a possible purchase of Portuguese territories,
and a vast communications network as far as Egypt. It was not unusual,
of course, for colonial politicians to dream of regional expansion in the

name of empire or to succumb to the blandishments of the imperial metropolis without necessarily subscribing to ideas of closer formal links with Great Britain. But Rhodes was at the centre of a powerful financial complex of mining and agricultural interests which generated the means to carry schemes through without committing Liberals or Conservatives to extra expenditure.

From this conjunction of imperial and colonial interests there operated an uneasy system of patronage funded by the extraordinary development of mining at Kimberley, and enshrined in the imperial honours lists for colonial politicians and in the university degrees that brought Rhodes to Oxford in 1899, or Sir Ernest Oppenheimer to Oxford in 1952, when Sir Maurice Bowra emphasized the continuity between the great amalgamator and his successor who 'made a combination of all the producers, putting, as it were, a ring of diamonds round the earth'.[57]

But the real patrons in this association were the colonials. When one keeps in mind the relative poverty of Oxford at the turn of the century, when an Endowment Fund started by Curzon managed an investment of only £24,989 by 1908 and had only the Gladstone Professorship to its credit by 1914,[58] the gifts of Rhodes, Beit (who left still greater sums to South Africa), and Sir Julius Wernher who helped found Imperial College, were major contributions towards the funding of overseas students and studies of the outside world. One cannot help agreeing, however reluctantly, with Milner that Oxford was extremely fortunate to gather crumbs, even whole loaves, from the tables of tycoons who were engaged in exploiting the imperial connection. The more cynical might agree with the view of Goldwin Smith who deplored 'the adoption of Oxford as a pedestal for a trophy of Cecil Rhodes'.[59] But that would be an extreme view of the connection — as extreme as the heady ambition to make Oxford an 'imperial university' which was a piece of conceit from those who had an Oxford-centred view of how patronage was, in fact, being dispensed.

The Rhodes and Beit bequests, however, did confer real advantages: firstly by an inflow of talent which in Beare's scheme would have been more widely dispersed; and secondly by a concentration of historical resources for those interested in the development of imperial connections and peripheral autonomy. Both Rhodes and Beit were closely involved in the dynamic changes in one of the most important colonial economies of the late Victorian empire. It is fitting that some of the capital accumulated from the diamond pits enables Oxford to further an understanding of such men and how they worked.

Notes

1. Milner Papers (Bodleian Library), dep. 468, Rhodes to Grey, 25 August 1901.

2. *Greater Britain*, no. 7 (15 May 1891), pp. 406-7; see, too, reports of his opinions and movements in *Imperial Federation. The Journal of the Imperial Federation League* (1 June 1892, 1 February 1893).

3. W.T. Stead, *The Last Will and Testament of C.J. Rhodes* (London, 1902).

4. Gordon Le Sueur, *Cecil Rhodes, the Man and his Work* (London, 1913); Phillip Jourdan, *Cecil Rhodes: His Private Life* (London, 1910); Sir Lewis Michell, *The Life of the Rt. Hon. C.J. Rhodes 1853-1902* (2 vols., London, 1910).

5. Basil Williams Papers, Rhodes House Library, MSS Afr. s. 134. Merriman to Williams, 10 April 1914, and notes of interviews.

6. Stead, *The Last Will*, p. 66.

7. J.G. Lockhart and C.M. Woodhouse, *Cecil Rhodes: The Colossus of Southern Africa* (New York, 1963), ch. 27 and p. 463.

8. Frederic Whyte, *The Life of W.T. Stead* (2 vols., London, 1925).

9. Basil Williams, *Cecil Rhodes* (London, 1921).

10. Ibid., p. 327.

11. Basil Williams Papers, Merriman to Williams, 4 July 1919.

12. F.J. Dormer, *Vengeance as a Policy in Afrikanderland* (London, 1901); William Plomer, *Cecil Rhodes* (London, 1933); Felix Gross, *Rhodes of Africa* (London, 1956).

13. Lockhart and Woodhouse, *Cecil Rhodes.*

14. John Flint, *Cecil Rhodes* (London, 1976). See, too, Jean van der Poel, *The Jameson Raid* (Cape Town, 1951); Denys Rhoodie, *Conspirators in Conflict: A Study of the Johannesburg Reform Committee and its Role in the Conspiracy against the South African Republic* (Cape Town, 1967); John S. Galbraith, *Crown and Charter. The Early Years of the British South Africa Company* (University of California, 1974).

15. A.P. Cartwright, *The Corner House* (Cape Town, 1965); *Gold Paved the Way* (Cape Town, 1967); G. Blainey, 'Lost Causes of the Jameson Raid', *The Economic History Review*, XVIII (1965), pp. 350-66; A. Jeeves, 'Rand Capitalists and the Coming of the South African War, 1896-1899', *Canadian Historical Papers* (1973), pp. 61-83; Robert V. Kubicek, *Economic Imperialism in Theory and Practice. The Case of South African Gold Mining Finance 1866-1914* (Duke University Press, 1979). For the diamond fields' period of his career, see Colin Newbury, 'Out of the Pit: The Capital Accumulation of Cecil Rhodes', *The Journal of Imperial and Commonwealth History*, IX, 4 (1981), pp. 25-49.

16. Newbury, 'Out of the Pit'.

17. Printed in Flint, *Cecil Rhodes*, Appendix, pp. 248-52.

18. Michell, *Life*, vol. I, pp. 83-4.

19. Oxford Union Library, 'Rough Minute Books', 1873-6; 1876-84.

20. Flint, *Cecil Rhodes*, p. 23.

21. Williams, *Cecil Rhodes*, pp. 41-2, 50.

22. Milner Papers, dep. 25, Milner to Stead, 15 November 1884; Milner to Matheson, 18 November 1884.

23. C.E. Mallet, *A History of the University of Oxford* (Oxford, 1927). Milner did, however, join in this toil.

24. Basil Williams Papers, Notebook I, f. 164.

25. I base this view on correspondence from Rhodes in the Hildersham Hall Papers, Rhodes House, MSS. Afr. s. 1647, which supplement the letters in MSS. Afr. s. 115. See, too, the valuable articles linking Herbert Rhodes with Elton by Norman A. Etherington, 'Labour Supply and the Genesis of the South African

Confederations in the 1870s', *Journal of African History*, 20 (1979), pp. 235–53; and 'Frederic Elton and the South African Factor in the Making of Britain's East African Empire', *The Journal of Imperial and Commonwealth History*, IX, 3 (1981).

26. For the earliest balances of his estate, Milner Papers, dep. 475, and the Trust correspondence in dep. 467; and for a preliminary list of his liabilities and assets and shares in companies, Newbury, 'Out of the Pit', Appendix III.

27. Galbraith, *Crown and Charter*, pp. 84–6.

28. Newbury, 'Out of the Pit', p. 39.

29. The reserve scheme and resistance by other directors to Rhodes's use of this collateral can be pieced together in the Rhodes Papers, Rhodes House MSS Afr. s. 228, De Beers C 7 A.

30. Ibid., Stow to Craven, 6 October 1890; Stow to Rhodes, 24 October 1890; Stow to Rhodes, 3 December 1891. Total value of the clandestine shipments and sales amounted to just over £500,000 which was declared and audited for the benefit of the board, before being added to the normal reserves.

31. Harcourt MS., Bodleian Library, dep. 387, October–November 1892.

32. Ibid., 31 October 1892.

33. Rhodes Papers MSS. Afr. t. 5, Rhodes to Parkes, 9 May 1895.

34. Harcourt MS. dep. 388, 24 November 1892.

35. Rhodes Papers MSS. Afr. s. 288, De Beers Mines C 7 A, Beit to Rhodes, 1 July 1893.

36. *Greater Britain,* 15 October 1892; Rhodes House MSS. Afr. t. 10, Elton Papers, Banks to Elton, 11 September 1955. Some of the credit for uncovering the sequence of the colonial scholarships scheme must go to L.B. Frewer, Superintendent of Rhodes House Library, who has left a minute on the topic with the Elton Papers. Sir Thomas Hudson Beare studied at London University on a South Australian government scholarship and became Professor of Engineering at University College and Edinburgh University. A copy of his reprint 'Britannic Scholarships' is in the Elton Papers.

37. Beare, 'Britannic Scholarships', pp. 6–7.

38. Rhodes House MSS. Afr. t. 10, J. Astley Cooper to Amery, 7 June 1925.

39. Rhodes House MSS. Afr. t. 1.

40. Oxford University Archives, 'Hebdomadal Council Register, 1879–1896', f. 420; *Hebdomadal Council Papers* (1891, 1892), Acts, 14 November 1892, Item 8. I am grateful to Mr T.H. Ashton, Keeper of the Archives, for permission to use these records.

41. Harcourt MS. dep. 387, 15 November 1892.

42. Rhodes House, Miscellaneous Papers MSS. Afr. s. 8, ff. 40–44. Balliol opposition predominated with eighteen signatures, but fifteen colleges were represented in the protest.

43. On 23 June D.B. Monro wrote to Arthur G. Butler, Fellow of Oriel and one of Rhodes's old tutors, explaining in detail the college's need for a capital grant of more than £80,000 to extend buildings, increase fellowship stipends and pay for Exhibitioners. This letter looks like an answer to a request by Butler on how a gift from Rhodes might be used. Butler appears to have kept in touch with Rhodes and later sent congratulations on the relief of Kimberley. Rhodes Papers, MSS. Afr. s. 228, C 28 Personal.

44. Milner MS. dep. 185, Beit to Milner, 7 August 1901.

45. Details of the 'sub-trust' are in Milner MS. dep. 475, 476. Milner also thought that political action outside South Africa might be supported 'in exceptional circumstances' and if the trustees were in agreement: Milner to Michell, 8 August 1914.

46. Milner MS. dep. 468, Rhodes to Hawksley, July 1899.

47. Ibid., dep. 467, f. 228; Parkin to Milner, 14 November 1902.
48. Oxford University Archives, W.P.B. 11 (12), Beit to Monro, 27 June 1904.
49. Milner MS. dep. 468, Michell to Milner, 6 October 1909.
50. Ibid., dep. 470, Michell to Milner, 20 March 1916.
51. Ibid., dep. 470, Michell to Milner, 7 December 1915.
52. Ibid., Milner to Michell, 31 December 1915.
53. Ibid., Wylie to Milner, 26 March 1916.
54. Ibid., Milner to Chamberlain, 22 June 1916.
55. Ibid., dep. 473, Minutes, 16 December 1924 (present Beit, Lovatt, Kipling, Amery).
56. See, for example, Rhodes Papers, MSS. Afr. s. 228, Charter 3 B, for a draft letter from Grey to the Vice-Chancellor proposing a bequest of £1,000 by Rhodes to fund a prize poem or essay on the empire: 'In spite of all he has done the impression still exists in certain quarters that he is a rather self-interested Afrikander than a disinterested Englishman.' (dated June 1895).
57. Anthony Hocking, *Oppenheimer and Son* (Johannesburg, 1973), p. 271.
58. Milner MS. dep. 487, Oxford Endowment Fund.
59. Smith to Bryce, 4 January 1903, cited in Max Beloff, *Britain's Liberal Empire*, vol. I (London, 1969), p. 43.

5 LIONEL CURTIS AND THE IDEA OF COMMONWEALTH

Deborah Lavin

Lionel Curtis was the prophet and evangelist of the new Commonwealth. He was not the creator of the concept, despite his claim, quoted by Sir Keith Hancock in the *Survey of British Commonwealth Affairs*:

> I came to think that the British Empire stood for something very different from the 'dominion over palm and pine', that its function in the world was to promote the government of men by themselves. . . . The upshot was that I came to regard the word 'Empire' as a misnomer. Hunting about for a good Saxon word to express the kind of state for which it stood I naturally lit on the word 'Commonwealth'.[1]

The liberal concept of 'Commonwealth', so far as it concerned the Greater Britain overseas, goes back beyond Goldwin Smith, and was as familiar to Rosebery and to John X. Merriman, to Freeman and to Zimmern, as it was to Curtis and to Hancock. Hancock was later to salute Curtis as the father of the *Survey*, but Curtis has usually been taken to be significant less on his own account than as a member of the study group that caused Lloyd George to comment that the empire was taking over Downing Street. The Round Table was a distinguished unofficial Edwardian think-tank, among whose members Robert Brand (the international banker) was better known than Curtis, and Philip Kerr (Lord Lothian, who worked on Lloyd George's staff, became Secretary to the Rhodes Trust and later Ambassador to Washington) was more apparently influential.[2] Curtis, after all, held official positions only twice in his life – for short periods in South Africa after the South African War and in the Colonial Office at the time of the Irish Treaty – and his idea of the Commonwealth never commanded general acceptance. The modern Commonwealth of national entities has turned out to be a far cry from his dream of a supra-national world state in which particularity would wither away. Yet Curtis stood in a special relation to its growth. He propagated the multinational Commonwealth and was, I believe, the first to explore in any detail the ideal of multiracial Commonwealth.

He preferred Oxford to Westminster as the centre of his activities, launching study groups and research projects designed to complement the activities of the Royal Institute of International Affairs at Chatham House, for the foundation of which he was largely responsible. His relation to Oxford was always equivocal. His fellowship of All Souls, which ran from 1923 to 1955 and included a stint as Sub-Warden, was much criticized, and his publications were notable for polemic rather than analysis. Yet he alerted an Oxford generation to empire, and inspired many to imperial service and study, both contemporary and historical. More than any other Oxford figure connected with empire, Curtis spanned its modern history from the emergence of the Commonwealth idea through its multiracial evolution. The religiosity of his concept of a *'civitas dei'* permeated the distinctive Oxford school of empire historiography into the 1930s and 1940s.

In 1955, shortly before his death, he attended his last meeting of the Ralegh Club in Oxford to hear Freddie Madden ask the question 'What is left of "the Empire of the Bretaignes"?' Curtis would have been gratified, but unsurprised, to hear the same speaker four years later persuade the Club to accept at last a new toast: 'The Commonwealth of Nations'. He had, after all, confidently predicted the capitulation and in the past had done much himself to promote it, although in his latter years he was anticipating the still remoter horizon of a single world government.

Curtis's undergraduate career at New College had been remarkable less for academic success in Greats (in which he attained a third) than for the contacts he made. He and a number of his contemporaries went on to participate in the Kindergarten's celebrations of the Mallard and the birthday of William of Wykeham among the tin shanties and Baker mansions of Johannesburg in 1901. But when Milner returned from South Africa in 1905, disappointed of his hopes of reconstruction and pessimistic about the future of empire, his *chelas*, inspired by the ideal he had held out to them, stayed on to become actively concerned with the evolution of South African Union. They formed themselves into a standing reading party (called the Moot to suggest antique populism allied to the Oxford virtue of discussion), studying appropriate federal constitutions to produce factual information. With the approval of Milner's successor, Lord Selborne, they began to sound out the politicians. It was too effective a combination to disband willingly even after Union had been achieved. For Curtis, who could not share Milner's pessimism, new horizons had been presenting themselves as early as

1907. He wrote to Selborne:

> It begins to dawn on one that South Africa is a microcosm and much
> that we thought peculiar to it is equally true of the Empire itself. We
> want some clear and coherent scheme before men's minds of what
> the Empire can be and should be. When we have done all we can do
> and should do for South Africa it may be we shall have the time and
> training to begin some work of the same kind in respect of Imperial
> Relations.[3]

Here for him lay the kernel of the 'imperial problem', needing only to
be properly formulated to be well on the way to resolution.

In 1909 Milner chaired a series of discussions on the future of the
empire, out of which grew the Round Table movement whose members
aimed at studying and then working towards imperial organic union.[4]
'The problem', as they saw it, grew out of a pragmatic assessment of
whether the continuation of empire was compatible with the growth
of nationalism. The achievement of self-government had confused the
old identities in the Dominions and had divided the nationalists, ex-
posing the contradictions between the Dominion claim to sovereignty
and the imperial reality which left foreign policy and defence to the
United Kingdom. From the British point of view, imperial defence was
dangerously over-extended, and relations between the constituent parts
of the empire were vulnerable because they were undefined. European
alignments had made defensiveness a habit of mind in Britain, and it
seemed necessary to determine whether the historic disruption of 1776
could be prevented from recurring now that the empire was again
under strain.

The Round Table considered existing alternatives and dismissed
them. Agreements such as had been proposed at the recent Imperial
Defence Conference could give no guarantee of long-term stability
because they were susceptible to change in the political authority of the
governments which had contracted them. They agreed that Richard
Jebb's alliance system, outlined in his study of colonial nationalism,
might do even more damage by projecting the tensions of international
politics into an already fissile empire. Their South African experience
predisposed the members of the Round Table to endorse Curtis's
precept that defining fundamental principle gave direction to subsequent
action. Where, they asked, did sovereign power in the empire lie – in
local autonomy or central authority? Their South African efforts, and
F.S. Oliver's interpretation of American history,[5] suggested a federated

empire as a constructive way round the dilemma. A new body, representative of the Dominions and conveniently removed from the vagaries
of party, would assume parliament's duties to the empire; from this
new imperial parliament would be drawn an imperial government at
the centre of the federation. It would be 'constitutionally responsible
to all the electors of the empire, and with the power to act directly
on individual citizens' (Kerr's formula): not federation merely, but full
organic union although as yet 'the only organisms which the British
empire resembles are the most primitive living objects whose only
method of growth and reproduction is to split in half' (Brand's verdict).[6]
The new organic union would combine domestic particularism with
internationalism. Each component state would continue to control its
own domestic affairs absolutely, while the imperial parliament would
provide a shared central direction of foreign policy and of trusteeship in
the dependencies, thus at once enhancing the international status of
the Dominions and ensuring the future of the Commonwealth. That
was to be the group's objective. Meanwhile, they thought, defence or
tariff agreements, though insufficient in themselves, would prepare
public opinion throughout the empire to face at last the logical alternatives long ago enunciated by Lord John Russell: was the British
empire to unite or dissolve?

With Milner's moral support and the finances of Lord Anglesey and
Abe Bailey to sustain them, the group extended their successful South
African strategy to the empire at large — a quarterly review (the *Round
Table*) to deal with imperial news and commentary, a secretariat to
collect, digest, and distribute information, Dominion groups to discuss
the scheme, and, as Philip Kerr put it, 'to shout "haroon" in a spon-
taneous manner when the egg is hatched'.[7] This time the egg (the
manifesto drafted by Curtis) was to be a definitive report on federation,
agreed and criticized by experts and timed to coincide with the 1911
Imperial Conference. Until it was published the movement was to be
non-political, even anti-political. But federation, baldly stated, was
hardly likely to gain an audience let alone seize the imperial public
by the ears, for all Milner's lobbying of the influential and the rich.
The new journal, when Kerr took it over, gave the movement standing;
but it needed the energy and enthusiasm of Curtis to enable it to take
flight, as Kerr recognized: 'I know no man who has so big a furnace
in his belly. It is so fierce that the fumes overwhelm his brain at times.
But it scorches all whom he encounters.'[8] Their first sortie into the
Dominions, a journey to Canada, depressed Philip Kerr and William
Marris but exhilarated Curtis, who returned 'far more hopeful than

when I started'.[9] His confidence prevailed; the group began to draft an imperial constitution while Curtis continued his Dominion journeys.

These completed Curtis's own moral conversion to the new imperialism, transforming it into an obsession. At thirty-eight he was still influenced by the sense of duty, often characteristic of evangelical Anglicanism, which inclined him to endow his work with portentous and pre-ordained significance:

> My task in life seems to be that of a pipe which collects the spare energies of a lot of people and concentrates them in one stream strong enough to generate electricity. If I married, much of the spare energies would go to waste for want of the pipe and turbine which I supply.[10]

Instinctively he answered his imperial problem not only in terms of his liberal education but in terms of his personal morality. Self-government was to him less a liberal constitutional formula than a moral proposition. An empire which existed to promote self-government rather than to perpetuate its own rule should more truly be called a Commonwealth, for its stability would lie not in alliances but in the acknowledged equality of its citizens (at present a mere fiction), giving them the sense of mutual duty which alone would commit them to the existence of the Commonwealth itself. This formulation of the question of citizenship was later to exercise other members of the Round Table — Coupland, who considered writing an extended study of the problem in 1920, and Zimmern, whose *Third British Empire* in 1925 posed the same question 'to what or to whom is a single allegiance due?'[11] To think merely in terms of an empire that was receding into the past would not have occurred to them, least of all to Curtis, for whom the international Commonwealth heralded the advent of nothing less than a *civitas dei*.

The moral earnestness with which Curtis applied himself to the study of empire was a compound of fundamentalist Christianity learned at home and idealist philosophy acquired at New College. When later he became disillusioned with the church, he moved confidently to propound in its place the moral state, the true Commonwealth, scandalizing Arnold Toynbee by posing the question, 'If Christ came back to earth, where, in the present day world, would he find that his precepts were best being practised?' and providing his own answer: the British Commonwealth.[12] From his reading of Hegel he had absorbed the working principle that the solution to any problem should be defined in the light of an ultimate object (to be revealed by faith and historical enquiry). From T.H. Green he derived his conviction that will rather than force is the basis of the state. Curtis defined freedom not as absence from constraint but as a social relation, and he transformed Green's proposition that 'among ourselves there is at least a potential duty of every man to every man' into an absolute of his own, constantly reiterated: 'the infinite duty of each to all'. If the self-governing Commonwealth was to be based on the mutual duty of all its citizens, then citizenship must be extended to all.

Curtis applied this proposition for the first time to the *international* state, using the modish imprecision of biological metaphor in which classes, races, and communities were united in an organic (as opposed to a democratic) state. His organism was not just a means of ensuring defence. It was to be 'a society in which every part is treated as something which must contribute to the benefit of the whole, from whose general welfare each part derives its own well being'.[13] Here Curtis's experience of Dominion self-government and colonial nationalism convinced him that the nature of the empire had been fundamentally changed. 'I cannot think of any one idea that has made such a deep impression on my own mind as your idea of Nationalism has done,' he wrote to Jebb[14] (a New College contemporary who was an associate in the study of the future of empire but propounded a solution very different from the organic union of the Round Table). The new imperial problem necessitated redefining 'centre' and 'periphery': no longer could domination from Westminster hold the empire together, or imperial issues be seen simply in terms of British interests. It had become necessary somehow to persuade the Dominions to collaborate with the United Kingdom in sharing the costs and maintaining the responsibilities of empire.

Curtis found, however, that definitive formulation of the problem proved unexpectedly intractable, and it was not until 1915 that the first part of his report, *Project of a Commonwealth*, was printed.[15] The Dominion Round Tablers, though interested, had been suspicious of any mission from London and were dubious of the details of the imperial parliament. To reassure them, Curtis emphasized that his scheme was merely a preliminary working hypothesis, to be modified by the results of dispassionate enquiry throughout the empire. This has been dismissed by many, then and since, as mere sophistry;[16] yet it is clear that in 1911 Curtis was not convinced that he had all the answers. He had made political blunders in the Dominions which he had retrieved as best he could but which made further political expression inopportune for a time. He had also become aware of a fundamental omission – the place of the dependencies – in his hypothesis:

> Now when I was in England I was sensible of a disinclination to touch the question of India and Egypt, but I tell you with the most absolute conviction, that we cannot possibly leave them out. We must face the question as to who is responsible for the great Dependencies under any new government which we put forward.[17]

On his return to Britain he found that the drafts of his report were apt 'to reduce people to a condition of terror', for the very reason that he was writing with the prejudices and opinions of the Dominions in mind. The whole balance between programme and action had to be thought out again, this time with the help of the universities.

He had been particularly struck by reading Arnold Toynbee's exposition of the role of the scholar citizens – 'men who shall be as students impartial, as citizens passionate'.[18] For Curtis, impartial enquiry and passionate advocacy often came to much the same thing in the end. It may well have been this quality which raised the suspicions of those scholars of Oxford who found his attitude to universities alarming:

> If we wanted to know what the constituents of the Empire were likely to accept we ought to have gone to the politicians and not, as we have consistently done, to the universities. . . . Ultimately it is imperative to know what people wish and decide but that will never be known until someone takes the trouble to find out what the real issues are and puts them in front of people in such a way that they can understand them. That is exactly the kind of work which Universities exist to do.

This was his answer to Keith Feiling, who enquired whether a university group was supposed to be producing an ideal constitution or a workable one.[19] Curtis and Kerr recruited two promising candidates for the Oxford Honour School of Modern History, and Curtis – characteristically monopolizing the more promising of the two, G.M. Paterson – set about approaching imperialists at the Universities of Cambridge, Reading, Birmingham, and Edinburgh to work on sections of the draft report. Early in 1912 the Oxford branch of the Round Table, with Coupland, Feiling, and Harold Prichard among its members, began a series of studies preliminary to compiling its own report on the imperial problem.[20] They endorsed Curtis's fundamental premise, that continuance of the empire in some form was desirable, and that it could not be maintained as it was. The members showed an encouraging preference for organic union, although they differed as to whether empire was a necessary condition for the status of the United Kingdom as a first-class power and were critical of the analysis of colonial nationalism, in response to which Curtis began to spell out his ideas on allegiance and citizenship.

By now he was recasting his report less as a prescription for a sort of systematic new imperialism than as a history of empire without which 'it is impossible for people really to see why having come into existence it deserves to be maintained'.[21] Most people, if they thought about the empire at all, thought of it in terms of English constitutional history, culled from books which

> dispose of the Unions of England with Scotland and Ireland in less than half a page and deal with the organization of a quarter of mankind in one international State as though it were nothing more than an episode of English history.[22]

Before the citizens of empire could be called upon to decide their future, it had become necessary to present them with a less anglocentric view of their past. He was reading copiously, though in the same manner as he listened — selectively, shaping what he learned into a weapon to be used in the service of the cause concerning him at the time. History revealed first principles and provided illustrations. Thus regarded, the Greek and Roman empires as interpreted by Zimmern or Freeman or Lucas showed that political aggregations were impotent unless informed by the basic principles of Commonwealth. On other, more modern, topics such authoritative research was often lacking. Murray Wrong was therefore set to tease out the fate of the American loyalists; Eustace Percy devilled on Germany. But, although Curtis's historical approach would cause any Oxford seminar then or since to shudder, he was concerned to draw his conclusions from the most authoritative sources possible. 'The work we are attempting is so colossal', he explained to Kerr, 'that we cannot afford to base it on shallow intellectual foundations.'[23]

He began purposefully to haunt Oxford. Rait of New College revised his chapter on the Union of Scotland, Adams and Grant Robertson worked on the British chapters; the Irish section (which Curtis was determined to include, despite the Moot's warnings) was mined from a nationalist, Lecky, and commented on by a Unionist, Seton. George Beer helped with America; perhaps most significantly of all for the future of the Oxford history school, the youthful Namier was converted to empire by Curtis and inspired to American research, which won him a Beit Prize and was to have been incorporated verbatim as an appendix to Curtis's report. Namier was nettled that it was not so included, but showed preoccupation with footnotes that exasperated the publishers. Instead, the Moot arranged the finance that allowed him to delay for many years writing *England in the Age of the American Revolution* and *The Structure of Politics in the Reign of George III.*[24] The historians were also driven out into the byways of imperial education. Zimmern and Namier were sent by the Moot to propagate their historical perspectives on the future of the empire in a series of lectures to the Workers' Educational Association (WEA) and Trade Union groups in Oxford, which drew from Namier a shocked comment on the ignorance they found, 'as complete concerning the white as the dark Empire'.[25] The history of the dependencies, indeed, caused Curtis considerable difficulty which he described to Philip Kerr:

> Is it really possible to interpret the relation of the self governing communities to the dependencies without some adequate historical treatment showing how those relations came into existence? No-one realises better than I the difficulty of preparing such an account and all I can do is to submit my work to historical authorities like Fisher.[26]

As he worked on it, this last problem came to outstrip all the others in its significance.

> The real difficulty is for us properly to realise the claims of the dependencies upon us, seeing that they are almost voiceless. . . . What has been brought home to me in these laborious researches is that the problem we have undertaken to study is not one of the problems of history but *the* problem . . . which arose when and because European civilisation began, and that is why I have found myself driven to go back to the beginning of things and to endeavour to explain them.[27]

In June 1912 Curtis was given the opportunity to formalize his association with Oxford. The electors to the Beit Lectureship rejected the applications of four other candidates and invited Curtis to take the post, recognizing the other calls on his time in the stipulation that he deliver not fewer than six lectures a term and reside in Oxford at least two days a week.[28] He was to work with H.E. Egerton, the first Beit Professor.

Egerton had not been disposed to criticize an empire he regarded as 'the most marvellous State ever conceived by the mind of man', to be appropriately studied by themes transcending 'mere local particularism' which would endow the subject with a 'dignity and a harmony ... otherwise lacking'. On rare occasions he was inspired to flights of fancy.

> Let our modest thank offering for the splended inheritance of our Imperial history be a reasonable and impartial mind to draw conclusions from evidence, before which the rhetoric and bluster of the mere partisan will wither and efface itself, like the snake-woman before the cold gaze of the Greek philosopher.[29]

More usually the fire burned low within him. The *Dictionary of National Biography* describes him austerely as 'never a popular lecturer, though serious students recognised him as a master of his field'. In their reports to the Hebdomadal Council recommending that the foundation be made permanent, Egerton and the first Beit Lecturer (W.L. Grant) adopted an apologetic tone both for the munificence of their endowment ('As a rule, a new Chair is established when a new study has to be provided for, for which there is an existing practical demand'), and for the response they had elicited.

> It has been my experience that to lecture on the internal history of a colony is to have a small audience, but that when the subject is linked up with the history of England, the audience increases. . . . In 1908–1910 [of a total audience of fourteen] twelve had the Schools in view; the other two were an Irishman who wished to see if the subject threw any light upon the question of Home Rule, and a Frenchman who wished to learn the secret of British colonial success.[30]

Egerton, a convinced though cautious federalist, later described his experience of Curtis's year as Beit Lecturer as having made him feel like a country rector with the Prophet Isaiah as his curate. He had deplored the fact that colonial history had not attracted students of real distinction: within a term Curtis had recruited some twenty regulars, including J.G. Lockhart, Vincent Massey, and Murray Wrong. Enthusiastic reports from Oxford confirmed that 'the new Imperialism has become a living force in the place'.[31] Curtis had settled with Egerton that his lectures should consist of extracts from his draft report to be duplicated and circulated to the students and later discussed on Friday evenings. In the Beit Seminar they beavered away on the details of financial provisions in the Australian and German federations; by the summer term his pupils were preparing papers for discussion by visiting experts on the implications of imperial union for the dependencies, foreign, military, and naval policy, with the active assistance of various Whitehall departments.[32] It was an education very much in the Oxford manner. His pupils would be invited, sometimes a dozen at a time, to stay at his house at Ledbury, where they had individual studies and bedrooms and learned to work to an unyielding schedule, punctuated by canoeing expeditions on the Wye. In the evenings there would be discussions with luminaries imported from London, civil servants or politicians.

> He wasn't preaching dogmatically. He was just being nice and friendly and trying to get to know what our ideas were. . . . It was all informal. It was the most perfect kind of public relations, of spreading ideas, that I've ever seen, but it was done deliberately. . . . He believed the way to spread a new idea was to capture the elite and convert them and they . . . would spread the ideas.[33]

Curtis was always kind to undergraduates in whom he divined promise, furthering their careers in ways that were advantageous to them and, incidentally, useful to himself. (Cammell Laird's, of which Hichens was the Chairman, became known as 'the home for lost Imperialists'.)[34]

On Sunday evenings the imperial net would be cast more widely in meetings of the Ralegh Club at which twenty-five members (later increased to over thirty) and their guests toasted 'the Empire of the Bretaignes' and discussed a paper on the politics of the British empire. Curtis and Hichens were the first Honorary Members. One of the prime movers in the Club's foundation in December 1912, J.G. Lockhart, described the meetings. The undergraduates smoked (churchwarden pipes were originally stipulated) and sprawled

> on the floor of some crowded room. . . . From time to time visits were paid by really big people, such as Cabinet Ministers and Proconsuls. . . . Of course they had not learnt the new language. Sometimes they would be a little 'jingo' and the converts (converts are so zealous!) would shudder with horror. And when they talked of

the Empire, the undergraduates, who knew better and called it the 'Commonwealth of Nations', would draw in their breath sharply, as though an infinitive had been split.[35]

There could be no more vivid illustration of the change of perspective that Curtis's lectureship had inspired. The Club's activities were not entirely confined to exploring the intricacies of imperial federation, though familiar themes cropped up among the early papers ('Is the British Empire worth maintaining?', 'The Federal Solution') and members of the Moot were prominent among the guests. Richard Jebb, speaking on 'The Britannic Commonwealth', received short shrift at the hands of the young Barrington-Ward for his advocacy of the Imperial Conference committees as the appropriate vehicle for conducting imperial affairs.[36] But many other topics showed that the Club was prepared to criticize aspects of existing imperial practice, nationalism, democracy, 'the need for a new Imperialism', the deficiencies of 'Doctrinair [sic] imperialism'. All looked to the possibility of what Lockhart called 'a moral basis of empire' rather than mere reiteration of federalism. More important still, a new consideration — the future of the dependencies — was discussed.

The terms of the Beit bequest had defined the subject with a heavy bias towards the history of the self-governing colonies, specifically including the old American colonies but ruling out India and the dependencies. These stipulations went unquestioned until 1934, when C.R.M.F. Cruttwell, Principal of Hertford, felt 'it might be held to exclude Colonial possessions other than our present Dominions', and the terms were adjusted — for a time — to 'the history and government of the British Empire'.[37] Reginald Coupland was to be the first Beit Professor to examine historical aspects of imperial race relations; appropriately, he addressed the Club's second meeting on 'the colour problem', arguing that, since it was an essentially modern phenomenon, it was not insurmountable. Much of the debate on Jebb's paper at the next meeting revolved round Jebb's view that 'to put dependencies under an Imperial Parliament would be bad for the dependencies and bad for the Parliament'.

This discussion reflected directly on the problem of imperial trusteeship and the dependencies which exercised Curtis's mind for much of 1912, after a series of Moot discussions of a paper by Philip Kerr on Indian representation in an imperial assembly. Curtis was not as yet propounding responsible self-government for India on the Dominion model, as he did some three years later. But he saw the question as the essential core of the whole imperial problem. It was a historic problem, in the relations between Europe and Asia; it raised the great moral question of the ultimate aim of British policy in the dependencies (which provoked dissension among the Round Tablers and was later to make Curtis extremely unpopular among civil servants and nationalists alike in India); most importantly it lay at the heart of the Moot's pragmatic reappraisal of the effects of Dominion, Irish, and Indian nationalism on the probable chances of holding the empire together. In the new circumstances, differences of view between the United Kingdom and the Dominions on questions like the exclusion of Indian immigrants or the treatment of indentured labour stood no chance whatever of being solved by action at Westminster. Such questions and all others touching the dependencies must, therefore, be removed to the new imperial assembly, where they would be considered by the constituents of the empire at large. Dominion nationalists might accept the change as completing their international status, while the promise of a voice in the regulation of constitutional change in the dependencies might reconcile them to the new assembly, in which their views would be modified by seeing for the first time the problem as it affected the empire as a whole. To the Indian nationalists it offered a modest degree of direct representation in the central council of the empire, where Gokhale might possibly act as a minister with or without portfolio.

On these matters the Round Table fought tooth and nail; only Curtis, among them all, raised the question of the other dependencies. Ceylon, Egypt, Malaya, West and East Africa might, he thought, send non-voting representatives, 'natives who were there not to rule but to criticize and inform', and 'who would bring before [the other representatives] the necessities of native life [as they] were never brought before a South African Assembly'.[38] This was an imaginative conception, transcending the initial idea of federal union, more original and more profound. Its controversial nature resulted in its exclusion from the published report, but in 1916 Curtis anticipated the Montagu Declaration by writing 'I should like to see the Imperial Constitution open ... with a preamble announcing that the Commonwealth exists for the purpose of extending self-government, as rapidly as may be, to all communities within its circle.' This view was the outcome of the logic of Curtis's moral assumptions. J.G. Lockhart commented that 'if you wanted to argue with Lionel Curtis you should vehemently dispute his opening proposition, for, that admitted, the rest of his case forms an unbreakable chain of logic'.[39] In Curtis's mind organic union demanded the presence of the dependencies; the principle of the Commonwealth demanded their inclusion as citizens; training in self-government anticipated their status as Dominions.

Such was the new imperialism discussed in the early years of the Ralegh Club, where for the first time in Oxford some of these matters were given a forum for vigorous debate. The annual dinners were star-studded occasions which Milner, E.D. Morel, and Churchill himself attended; prominent senior members of the university were among the regular guests. The Commonwealth became a recognized, even a respectable, Oxford Sunday evening preoccupation, like a Balliol concert.

The Colonial Club, whose members were Rhodes Scholars, was kept supplied with speakers by Curtis and Coupland in these years, but seems to have developed differently, judging by Hancock's reference to its later 'Rabelaisian extravagances'.[40] Nor did the Cambridge colony of the Ralegh develop the momentum of the Oxford original, despite its self-governing status. Coupland gave it a name, the Chatham Society (not to be confused with the Pitt Club; Coupland was editing Chatham's war speeches at the time); J.G. Lockhart gave the opening address and Curtis enlisted the sponsorship of Benians and Temperley.[41]

Curtis was careful to establish an approved succession to the Beit Lectureship before he resigned in 1913. Coupland was groomed for the office, his research expenses met by the Moot, and his rapid promotion to the Chair ensured by a strategy devised by Curtis. Often he was transported bodily to Ledbury, where Curtis would supervise his work and, at one remove, the seminar which met regularly in his rooms in Trinity to carry on the task of devising a new constitution for the empire. He acknowledged Curtis's efforts on his behalf handsomely:

> From 1912 I have always been in your debt . . . It was from *The Problem of the Commonwealth* and even more from the *Letter to the People of India* on Responsible Government that I discovered what political science really is.[42]

The Ralegh Club went into abeyance during the First World War, but, when Lockhart, Coupland, and Curtis revived it in 1919, it was with the hope of its being 'strong and influential in the study and formulation of general policies in the British Commonwealth and Empire'[43] and, as Coupland wrote to Grigg while he was editing the *Round Table*,

> mainly because when the [Moot] propaganda begins next year it will

need an Oxford vehicle: that is the Ralegh's job. Moreover, if we can have one or two really instructive meetings on the European situation, we shall get good audiences and extend our influence.[44]

The Club's progress between the wars is in many ways the story of Oxford's influence on and response to the development from empire to Commonwealth. This is not, perhaps, best judged by the time it took the Ralegh to toast in the silver loving-cup not 'the Empire of the Bretaignes' but 'the British Commonwealth'. For a few meetings the new toast was drunk in 1920, but it was abandoned by eleven votes to five in the first division in the Club's history. Coupland and the Commonwealth men fought a rearguard action in 1921 but, foreseeing defeat, withdrew their motion proposing 'The Commonwealth of Nations'.[45] (It was Balliol rather than Trinity which had taken up the name; the Commonwealth Club there, organized by G.E. Lavin and fostered by Curtis and A.L. Smith, was largely sustained by ex-service-men throughout the university but foundered in 1921.) The Ralegh did not take any more readily to the idea of multiracialism. In 1926 the Club's original membership of twenty-five was increased to thirty 'to render possible the election of members hailing neither from Great Britain nor from one of the Dominions, and so to make the Club more representative of the Empire as a whole'. One Maltese member was elected (E. Scicluna); and a member from Jamaica in the following year (N. Talbot Mais). But, though the first Indian Honorary Member was elected after speaking in 1930 (M.R. Jayakan, Member of the Indian Legislative Assembly and the British Indian Delegation), it was 1936 before Coupland first notified his intention of nominating Indian undergraduate members, and 1938 before A.W. Mahmood and C.B. Rao joined the Club.[46] As for women, it was easier for them to pass through the eyes of their own needles than to gain acceptance by the Bretaignes. Margery Perham (a pioneer in this as in much else) spoke on 'Trusteeship for Native Races in Africa' in 1933, but she was not accorded the status of Honorary Member until two years later, and she remained the only woman ever admitted to membership, a more liberal motion in 1936 being defeated by a large majority.[47]

In other ways, however, the Club did fulfil the expectations of its founders. In the inter-war years it considered the major developments in the empire — the Indian reforms, Middle and Far Eastern problems, Ireland, and developments in tropical Africa (which were comprehensively dealt with by Lugard, Guggisberg, Oldham, Clifford, and Cameron as well as Miss Perham). The Labour view of empire was expounded by Leonard Barnes; Commonwealth problems of defence, preference, and communications received attention. There was almost no consideration of the practice of foreign empires, and few specifically economic topics seem to have been discussed, but considerable emphasis was given to the British industrial outlook and the impact of Hitler. The Club was influential enough to draw first-rate speakers; it was popular, and its membership and guest lists show how often academics, politicians, administrators, and undergraduates met to discuss issues of current importance. It seems certain that the Ralegh should be included in any assessment of Oxford's impact on the making of policy in the years when 'middle opinion' in the heyday of its fashion brought the universities close to the sphere of public policy.[48]

After Curtis resigned the Beit Lectureship his association with Oxford continued through All Souls. For some years, in addition to his research work for the Round Table, he was unofficially connected with policy-making: in India at the time of the introduction of dyarchy in the Montagu-Chelmsford reforms, in Paris in the League of Nations' Section of the Peace Conference. For two years he joined the Colonial Office working in his capacity as a Dominions expert, advising on the suitability of a Dominion settlement in Ireland as Joint Secretary (with Tom Jones) of the British delegation, and then securing the Treaty's delicate political implementation. His new circumstances gave him a larger field within which to pursue familiar preoccupations – the need for national policy to be shaped by a conception of the universal interests of society at large and the necessity for an education of public opinion to keep the whole in view, the precondition for an educated public being 'a small number of people in real contact with the facts who had thought out the issues involved'.

At the Paris meetings in 1919 he had renewed old contacts, not only among the Dominions delegations but among the Americans – G.L. Beer (whom he recruited to the Section) and Whitney Sheppardson, one of the Balliol students who had fallen under his spell as Beit Lecturer, and who became one of Curtis's closest friends when he was the first Secretary to the Council of Foreign Relations and later the Rockefeller Foundation. In these encounters were suggested the ideas that resulted, largely through the work of Sheppardson and Curtis, in the parallel foundations of the Council on Foreign Relations and the Institute of International Affairs at Chatham House, for research and discussion of politics and international relations. From the beginning, the research aspect was emphasized in the preparation of a history of

the Peace Conference by Temperley and in the annual *Surveys* by
Arnold Toynbee.

Curtis was aware of the need to encourage a positive informed
American interest in empire, not merely as the basis of a new internationalism but to utilize American skills and American resources, and
he made a number of practical contributions to the new Anglo-
Americanism which took him into the American universities. At the
Williamstown (Mass.) Institute of Politics in 1922 he lectured on the
theme that

> all policies in the last analysis now turn on the mutual relations of
> the white races of Europe, America, and Australia to those of Asia
> and Africa. If this view is right then there can be no final achieve-
> ment in human affairs until these relations are made subject to law
> controlled by all the people concerned, in so far as they are fit to
> exercise such control.[49]

He invited Garfield, the Director of the Williamstown Institute, to All
Souls to encourage him to make Oxford the setting for the first joint
meeting of foreign affairs experts from the English speaking world in
1924. In the next year Curtis organized an international conference on
the new Commonwealth at Williamstown — with sessions on Commonwealth history, the Dominions, Ireland, India, tropical Africa, Egypt,
and the Middle East, the Dominions and foreign policy, and the
Commonwealth and the League.[50]

The emphasis on the dependent empire in this programme is significant. From about 1920 Curtis had become increasingly interested
in the problems of East Africa, co-operating with Oldham in represent-
ations to the government on the question of Northey's labour circulars,
and from this starting-point coming to consider the necessity for 'a full
comprehensive enquiry into the basic principles which ought to govern
our administration of primitive peoples in un-mandated territories of
the British Commonwealth under the direct administration of the
Colonial Office'.[51] Curtis was impressed by the arguments of MacGregor
Ross and Norman Leys ('the most formidable indictment of British
Colonial policy which has appeared for a century'[52]), but felt that the
very enunciation of the paramountcy principle, for which he had
campaigned, revealed new dangers:

> Our danger is that we are always enunciating unimpeachable prin-
> ciples without being prepared to face their practicable consequences.

> To run Kenya primarily for the benefit of the African population is the only sound principle, but the practical applications have never been faced.[53]

The political experience and research at Chatham House, contact with the American school of economic and sociological enquiry, and the plain need to investigate African problems more scientifically stimulated Curtis, together with Kerr and Coupland, to contemplate a scheme for reforming Oxford's approach to political science ('at the moment the subject is amateurish, unauthoritative and unorganised') in a new school of government based on All Souls, to study post-war international relations and to combine more effectively the elements of the Modern Greats degree — 'the study of the structure and the philosophical, political and economical principles of modern society'.[54] Smuts's Rhodes Memorial Lectures of 1929 persuaded them to propose a second project, a centre for African studies at Rhodes House, to support four research professorships, and to undertake research in co-operation with all the colonial administrations in Africa (except, it seems, Portugal). Both schemes foundered: All Souls had been unenthusiastic about the original project and flatly refused to contemplate 'the Africans'; the Rockefeller Foundation (approached officially by Kerr and unofficially by Curtis in 1930) confined its Oxford grant to saving the Bodleian Library. Something of the scheme was adopted by Abraham Flexner in his Institute for Advanced Studies at Princeton, on which he had consulted Curtis and Kerr.[55]

The African research project was not dropped, but came to assume a different form and was in the end attached to Chatham House, rather than to Rhodes House. As Curtis put the project to Keppel (of the Carnegie Foundation):

> This continent is now exposed to the impact of European civilisation which will ruin the life of its ... people unless it is controlled. In order to control it we must study not only the ideas, institutions, customs and languages, but the effects which an economic revolution is having on them in all its aspects ... We must learn what administrative activities, education and physical science directed by government and private agencies can do to enable them to gain instead of lose by the changes which are being forced upon them.[56]

What was needed, it seemed, was to state the African problem and to produce a Durham Report or an African Simon Commission to cover

Africa as a whole. Finding a Durham proved an exacting task. More than thirty candidates were considered before Curtis announced to the astonished Indian proconsul, Sir Malcolm Hailey, that the choice had fallen upon him. Curtis took Hailey round Addison's Walk to tell him about the need for the African inquiry. Hailey incautiously responded that it would be useful – but who would undertake it? 'Curtis stopped short, ... pulled up and turned to Hailey, pronouncing with finger outstretched, "Thou art the Man".'[57]

The African problem had been tackled: characteristically, Curtis made a rapid switch to the Oxford problem. The fate of the scheme for African studies at Oxford had made him realize that the 'chaotic' system of university finance needed 'the elementary principals [sic] of public finance which the younger Pitt introduced into the British exchequer at the end of the eighteenth century'.[58] A new study group was convened, including Roy Harrod, Arthur Salter, and a fresh recruit, H.V. Hodson, to produce *The Government of Oxford* (1931), which Curtis ensured attracted the attention of a leader in *The Times*.[59] He mobilized the antique Lord Grey, Chancellor of the University, and hounded an unenthusiastic Vice-Chancellor, Homes Dudden, into accepting a bargain from the erstwhile Rand magnate, R.W. ffennell, who offered the entire Wytham Estate to Oxford as 'one of the foremost universities of the world and one of the great centres of Imperial training and imperial thought'.[60] At the same time Grey and Homes Dudden found themselves sponsoring the Oxford Society, conceived by Curtis to harness the energies of Oxford's world-wide community and to provide a single continuing endowment 'not merely to preserve what Oxford had achieved, but also what she ought to be'.[61] It was a prime example of Curtis's tactics: 'imagination, dynamic concentration, a (rather deceptive) meekness of the dove with the (at first invisible) wisdom of the serpent'.[62] He found the members, fired off a missile at the Hebdomadal Council, drafted the society's constitution, organized its publication of *Oxford*, persuaded Waldorf Astor to launch it at a dinner at which Grey and Salisbury were to speak, and drafted their speeches. The effort was, in the last analysis, directed at the need for organized research (such as Cambridge had achieved in the sciences) in the field of politics, administration, anthropology, and government – 'the tap-root of Oxford thought'.

As to the study of government, let us remember how far its actual working throughout this vast Empire is in the hands of men trained at Oxford. How can Oxford properly train men for their work in

India, the Soudan, the Crown Colonies and the diplomatic services unless it is studying the facts with which they are to deal, and is drawing on the experience of those who are already dealing with them.[63]

His *coup de grâce* was to persuade a reluctant Arthur Salter to accept the Gladstone Chair of Political Theory and Institutions which W.G.S. Adams was about to vacate in 1932.

I was for a moment rather proud of myself for resisting what Lionel Curtis wished me to do, reflecting that neither I nor others had often succeeded in doing so. And then, somehow, I cannot to this moment recall how or why, I found myself at All Souls and a Professor in October.[64]

From his vantage point of All Souls Curtis had continued to preach the doctrine of Commonwealth to a new generation of young men. W.M. Macmillan has recalled in his autobiography how such attention as was paid to the African empire in 1920, when he first met Curtis and Kerr, came from two sources — the missionary bodies and 'the ideological imperialists'. Curtis, at this stage, had a foot in both camps, and seems to have approved Macmillan's early writings on the African predicament in South Africa. 'Mysterious as he was, I found Curtis a sympathetic figure, the one person to whom I spoke who came near to explaining my own sense of predestination and my somewhat visionary ideas of service to the colonial world.'[65] In 1923 Keith Hancock, too, fell prey to what he calls 'Curtis's human warmth and shrewd indoctrination'. He would play tennis at Curtis's Kidlington home ('on a court of hard earth, upheaved here and there by a pertinacious mole') or sleep in a Chatham House attic and breakfast on grilled herrings and mustard sauce with Curtis at the Oxford and Cambridge Club, while Curtis expounded the Irish Treaty or political reform in India. He recalls Curtis

sitting on a garden seat beneath the twin towers of the Hawksmoor Quad, when he exclaimed, 'Research! Research! I want all you young men to do research! No matter what conclusions you come to . . . Besides, I know what conclusions you *will* come to!'[66]

Curtis suggested that Chatham House should publish surveys of Commonwealth affairs to the high standards already achieved by

Toynbee's annual volumes, and was certainly influential in getting the first volume offered to Hancock, though it was Toynbee who made the approach. In retrospect, Hancock lays emphasis on the differences between his view of the Commonwealth and that of Curtis: his own political translation of the word, he says, involved not the imperial super-state but the common rituals and co-operative procedures of the family. He was, he claims, a Jebbusite; it was he who later encouraged J.D.B. Miller to write a study of Jebb.[67] Yet at the time the distinction was not, perhaps, so absolute. Hancock had persuaded Curtis to publish an edition of the *Selborne Memorandum*; and there is, surely, more than an echo of Curtis in the idea that

> Canadian history ceased to be provincial, its significance became universal and prophetic, when one discovered in it the emergent theory of the multi-national state. . . . No other theory contained any hope of reconciling the claims of unity and liberty . . . no other theory held hope for survival for the wide community of the Commonwealth, which must either pursue liberty, equality and fraternity amongst its constituent nations or perish in the conflict of nations.[68]

Hancock recognized the influence. He wrote of his *Survey* to Curtis:

> I wonder whether it made you feel fatherly? Of course, sons develop characteristics and attitudes distinct from those of their parents, but the real relationship is not shaken off. I wonder if you saw the relationship, of me to you, in my volume? It is there. Your thought is throughout the centre of reference, even when the reference is critical.[69]

By the mid-1930s Curtis was provoking strong criticism from those whom he had earlier influenced. He was now concerned less with the practical problems of imperial citizenship and nationalism from which his earlier imaginative ideas had sprung than with historical disquisitions and theological speculations. The three volumes of *Civitas Dei* (1934-7) ('a superb title', wrote Grant Robertson, 'which many alas will not be able to translate, but imagine it is something to do with Nankin or Gandhi or the Wafd or, more probably, the Ogpu')[70] aimed at nothing short of reconciling Christianity with empire, authority with the principle of Commonwealth on a world scale. All Souls was startled to learn that 'no political science can guide men far on their journey through life until it can say what is the goal to which the journey should lead';

that the study of international affairs demanded the recognition that 'the government of men by themselves' was nothing less than 'the guiding principle in public affairs'; that the British Commonwealth had become the key to 'the political structure of human society'.[71] Frank Underhill, who had described undergraduate life at Ledbury with such enthusiasm, thought the book

> a sad and disappointing culmination to a really useful career . . . Among imperialists he stood by himself, separated on the one side from the hard-boiled propagandists of the grosser type of commercial imperialism, the Chamberlains and the Amerys, and on the other side from the suave and over-polished casuits who professed to expound his own gospel of the Commonwealth, the Philip Kerrs and the Zimmerns.[72]

Curtis was unforgiving towards lapsed disciples, and the acrimony of the later years has, I believe, largely obscured the importance of the earlier associations. Coupland came to quarrel so bitterly with him that they were hardly on speaking terms; Macmillan upbraided him for concentrating on the Dominions to the exclusion of the colonies; Hancock declared himself to be 'at war with Curtis and Co. not only on issues of constitution-making and foreign policy but on the racial issue'.[73] Margery Perham clashed with him in *The Times* over the fate of the High Commission Territories; Kenneth Wheare accused him of not knowing a federation when he saw one.[74] In All Souls Curtis came to be regarded rather as the Ancient Mariner might have been, his Commonwealth now an albatross. Yet his attachment to both was undiminished. He came to contemplate his failures with perverse relish, claiming with some pride that for him to lend his name to any cause would lead to its inevitable demise.

In a perceptive essay, *Richard Jebb and the Problem of Empire* (written at the suggestion of Hancock), Bruce Miller concluded that the Commonwealth was, after all, the product of London rather than Oxford. 'The sort of Commonwealth that has emerged in the 1940s and 1950s bears the name that Curtis popularised, but has little else in common with what he envisaged. It is much closer to what Jebb hoped for.'[75] In the end, of course, it is neither. Miller's essay appeared in 1956, the year of the Suez crisis, when it became ironically clear that Jebb's concept of imperial alliance was if anything less realistic than Curtis's predicted alternatives of imperial unity or disintegration. Jebb dismissed 'any parallelism whatever between the connection of

England with India and the other dependencies on the one hand, and with the colonial States on the other',[76] whereas Curtis's logical pursuit of his initial premise led him to explore and to encourage others in the profoundly original idea that multiracial Commonwealth was not only a moral duty but practical politics. By 1914 Jebb's voice on empire was muted: Curtis was then at the beginning of his career in Oxford. Many of his Oxford converts went on to pursue the multiracial idea of Commonwealth further than he did himself: Curtis left them standing as he fixed his prophetic gaze on the realization of the kingdom of God on earth. There they refused to follow him; yet something of his influence was still to be seen in the idea of the empire created in the wartime Ministry of Information by H.V. Hodson and by Vincent Harlow, who wrote in *The Character of British Imperialism*,

I believe that the sociological concept which has slowly emanated from British overseas experience is capable of making an important contribution to a process by which the human race may bridge the canyon between national anarchy and a new world order. By that dangerously elusive phrase . . . I mean world government.[77]

Notes

1. Curtis to W.K. Hancock, 9 January 1935, quoted in W.K. Hancock, *Problems of Nationality, 1918-1936* (*Survey of British Commonwealth Affairs*, vol 1) (London, 1937), p. 54, n. 1.

2. See John E. Kendle, *The Round Table Movement and Imperial Union* (Toronto, 1975).

3. MS Selborne 71, Curtis to Selborne, 18 October 1907.

4. Maud Selborne Papers, Bodleian Library MSS Eng. Hist. c 1007, Memo of conversations which took place between a few English and South African friends at intervals during the summer of 1909, confidential, almost certainly by Lionel Curtis, pp. 19-26; account written by Lord Wolmer, 5 September 1909, pp. 28-37; memo. by Lord Howick, 8 September 1909, pp. 38-45.

5. F.S. Oliver, *Alexander Hamilton: An Essay on American Union* (London, 1906).

6. Memorandum, *Aim of Moot, January 1910*, quoted in Deborah Lavin, 'History, Morals and the Politics of Empire' in John Bossy and Peter Jupp (eds.), *Essays Presented to Michael Roberts* (Belfast, 1976), p. 120.

7. Lothian Papers, Edinburgh, GD40/17/2, Kerr to Curtis, 31 August 1910.

8. Quoted, without reference, in J.R.M. Butler, *Lord Lothian* (London, 1960), p. 38.

9. Maud Selborne Papers, MS Eng. Lett. c 456/126, Curtis to Lady Selborne, 30 December 1909.

10. MSS Eng. Hist. c 430/135, Curtis to Lady Selborne, 18 August 1910.

11. A Zimmern, *The Third British Empire* (London, 1934 ed.), p. 4.

12. A Toynbee, *Acquaintances* (Oxford, 1967), p. 146.

13. MS Curtis, Curtis to Kerr, 13 November 1916 (written from India) private.

14. Jebb Papers, London, Curtis to R. Jebb, 31 December 1906.

15. It was published in 1916 as *The Commonwealth of Nations*. A more popular version, *The Problem of the Commonwealth*, was published under Curtis's name in the same year.

16. 'Janitor' (J.G. Lockhart and M. Lyttelton), *The Feet of the Young Men* (London, 1928), p. 177.

17. MSS Eng. Hist. c 870, Curtis to F.S. Oliver, 13 August 1910 (copy).

18. A. Toynbee, *The Industrial Revolution of the Eighteenth Century in England* (London, 1908), p. 192.

19. MSS Eng. Hist. c 793, Curtis to Feiling, 20 February 1912.

20. Ibid., report of the Oxford Group, 25 March 1912 (revised 7 June 1912).

21. Curtis to E.J. Kylie, 10 January 1913, quoted in Lavin, 'History, Morals and the Politics of Empire', p. 123.

22. Curtis, *The Problem of the Commonwealth*, p. 228.

23. MSS Eng. Hist. c 806/110, Curtis to Kerr, 12 January 1912. For further consideration of Curtis's approach to history, see Lavin, 'History, Morals and the Politics of Empire'.

24. MSS Eng. Hist. c 807, Curtis to E. Grigg, 25 October 1913; Grigg to Curtis 16 and 17 October 1913; Curtis, Memo about Namier's Essay.

25. MSS Eng. Hist. c 786, Namier to Grigg, 14 July 1914.

26. MSS Eng. Hist. c 806/142, Curtis to Kerr, 2 March 1912.

27. See n. 21 above.

28. Minute book of the Beit Trust, 29 June 1912. I should like to thank Mr J. Brown, Secretary to the Managers of the Beit Fund, for showing me these records. See too MS Milner dep. 32/297-300, 'Candidates for Beit Professor'.

29. H.E. Egerton, 'On some Aspects of the Teaching of Colonial History', *United Empire*, 2 (1911), pp. 345, 348.

30. Report to Council by Hugh Edward Egerton, January 1911; Report by Mr W.L. Grant, Beit Lecturer, 1906-10; both in minute book of the Beit Trust.

31. MSS Eng. Hist. c 793, G.M. Paterson to P. Horsfall, 14 March 1913.

32. Ibid., papers to be read and discussed, summer 1913; MSS Eng. Hist. c 806, Curtis to Miss Bannatyne, 5 September 1912.

33. Transcript of interview with Frank Underhill, by courtesy of W.D. Meikle, Maberly, Ontario.

34. MSS Eng. Hist. c 794, J.G. Lockhart to E. Grigg, 29 August 1913.

35. 'Janitor', *The Feet of the Young Men*, p. 178.

36. Ralegh Club minute book, 5th meeting, 11 May 1913. I should like to thank Professor Kenneth Kirkwood for permission to consult these papers.

37. C.R.M.F. Cruttwell to the Registrar, 2 October 1934. File: 'Beit Professorship and Fund', see n. 28.

38. MSS Eng. Hist. c 826, Curtis, Note on Philip Kerr's Indian Memorandum (1912).

39. 'Janitor', *The Feet of the Young Men*, p. 175.

40. W.K. Hancock, *Country and Calling* (London, 1954), p. 83.

41. MSS Eng. Hist. c 794, F.S. Oliver to E. Grigg, 24 February 1914; R. Coupland to Grigg, 4 March 1914; see ᵢ   is to Grigg, 9 February 1914.

42. MS Curtis 116, R. Coupland tc   23 November 1937.

43. Giles Alington, Dean of University College, speaking on Coupland's death, Ralegh Club minutes, 9 November 1952.

44. MSS Eng. Hist. c 794, Coupland to Grigg, 4 November 1914.

45. Ralegh Club minutes, 2 May 1920, 20 November 1921 and 26 February 1922.

46. Ibid., 30 January 1938.

47. Ibid., 5 March 1923, 27 October 1935, 3 May 1936.

48. See A. Marwick, 'Middle Opinion in the 1930s: planning, progress and political "agreement" ', *English Historical Review* (1964).

49. MSS Eng. Hist. c 872, Summary of lectures, July-August 1922.

50. MS Curtis 3, Synopses of Williamstown Conference, July-August 1925.

51. Oldham Papers, box 238 (old classification), Curtis to Joseph Oldham, 11 November 1920.

52. MSS Eng. Hist. c 872, Curtis to Whitney Sheppardson, 1 January 1925.

53. Oldham Papers, box 240 (old classification), Curtis to Oldham, 30 January 1924.

54. Oldham Papers, box 240 (Curtis file), Curtis to Oldham, 23 January 1924 (private).

55. Lothian Papers GD 40/17/142, 160, A. Flexner to Curtis, 7 April 1926 and Kerr to Flexner, 13 May 1926 (private).

56. Lothian Papers GD 40/17/121, Curtis to Keppel, 20 July 1931.

57. W.M. Macmillan, *My South African Years* (Cape Town 1975), p. 243.

58. MS Curtis 102, Curtis to the Vice-Chancellor (Homes Dudden), 18 January 1931.

59. Ibid., Curtis to G. Dawson, 1931.

60. Ibid., notes by R.W. ffennell, *Preservation of the Wytham Estate*, 9 February 1931.

61. Ibid., Curtis to Lord Grey of Fallodon, 5 August 1930.

62. Lord Salter, *Memoirs of a Public Servant* (London 1961), pp. 238-9.

63. MS Curtis 102, draft speech for Lord Grey by Lionel Curtis.

64. Salter, *Memoirs*, p. 239.

65. Macmillan, *My South African Years*, p. 199.

66. W.K. Hancock to the author, 17 July 1979.

67. J.D.B. Miller, *Richard Jebb and the Problem of Empire* (University of London, Institute of Commonwealth Studies, Commonwealth Papers III, 1956).

68. Hancock, *Country and Calling*, pp. 161-2.

69. MS Curtis 11, Hancock to Curtis, 23 September 1937.

70. MS Curtis 112, Grant Robertson to Curtis, 27 March 1934.

71. L.G. Curtis, *Civitas Dei* (3 vols., London, 1934-7), vol. I, p. 284.

72. MS Curtis 151, Underhill, Review of *Civitas Dei* in *Canadian Forum* (August 1934).

73. Hancock to the author, 17 July 1979.

74. M. Perham and L. Curtis, *The Protectorates of South Africa, The Question of their Transfer to the Union* (Oxford, 1935); Sir Kenneth Wheare in conversation with the author, 1977.

75. Miller, *Richard Jebb*, p. 48.

76. R. Jebb, *Studies in Colonial Nationalism* (London, 1905), pp. 276-7, quoted in Miller, *Richard Jebb*, pp. 33-4.

77. MS Curtis 110.

6 MARGERY PERHAM AND COLONIAL ADMINISTRATION: A DIRECT INFLUENCE ON INDIRECT RULE

Anthony Kirk-Greene

This chapter attempts to evaluate an institutional influence through the medium of a single person. It asks what was the influence of Margery Perham, tutor and later Reader in Colonial Administration at Oxford from 1924 to 1948, and active in the teaching field for another fifteen years beyond, on the professional thinking and action of several hundreds of District Commissioners, both in the making and those back for more, whom she taught and talked with; and what was her influence on the shaping of colonial policy along the corridors of Whitehall and Westminster, as well as along the Secretariat and Government House verandahs from Ashanti and Accra across to Zomba and Zanzibar. Above all, the paper addresses itself to the question of what exactly was the Oxford dimension, projected through the intellectual evangelism of Margery Perham, to that special aspect of colonial administration with which her name will always be linked: indirect rule.

Margery Freda Perham was born in Lancashire in 1895, the second daughter and youngest child of seven.[1] Her father was a prosperous merchant in Harrogate, her mother of French stock. On going down from St Hugh's, Oxford, towards the end of the First World War, she took a lectureship at Sheffield University. Here she found that the strain of a depleted staff, dealing with a large number of ex-soldiers, 'many of them restless and poorly qualified academically', was too much. She had a breakdown and was given a year's leave of absence. To recover from this, in 1922 she went, 'rather indefensibly' (her mother wanted to take her to a luxury hotel in the Lake District) to Africa, to stay with her elder sister Ethel, who had married a District Commissioner in British Somaliland.[2] In 1924, after 'an internal convulsion . . . which shook the whole university', Margery Perham was back at Oxford, as Fellow and Tutor in Modern History and Modern Greats at her old college, St Hugh's. In keeping with the Oxford tradition of lecturing on more or less what you like once you have obtained your lectureship, she offered a course of lectures on the League of Nations and on what she called 'British Native Policy'. In 1929 she was awarded a Rhodes Travelling Fellowship, to study 'Native Problems'. 'I have never understood', she reflected, 'what suddenly brought to me, a young and obscure female don, in a period in which women had a very secondary status in Oxford, the offer.' And round the world she went, well before the days of air travel, to America, across the Pacific to Fiji and New Zealand, and then to Africa. In Tanganyika a crisis confronted her. Two cables arrived. One from Philip Kerr, Secretary of the Rhodes Trust, offered her a further year of travel. The other, from the Principal of St Hugh's, warned her that if she accepted that offer she would be required to resign her fellowship. She sent off two one-word cables: 'Accept' and 'Resign'. 'I now had to sit down and consider as calmly as I could how best to use this glorious gift of time.' That, too, was to be answered in one word: Africa.

On her return to a generous St Hugh's in 1930 she was appointed Research Fellow, but her college was not to be the priority among her interests. In 1931 she spent nine months away in Nigeria. In 1932 she was off again, this time to the Sudan, on a Rockefeller Travelling Fellowship. For this, it seems, the least welcome *quid pro quo* was having to sit in on Malinowski's seminar at the London School of Economics. 'There, as the only student of history and colonial government, I had to endure being the butt of the master ... I was generally sinking out of my depth in the dark swamps of anthropology.' In 1935, with her case canvassed by Coupland and Stallybrass, she was appointed Research Lecturer in Colonial Administration, and four years later the university recognized her contribution by electing her as its first Reader in that subject. To this post in 1945 was added briefly the Directorship of Oxford's Institute of Colonial Studies. Nuffield College had already elected her an Official Fellow in Imperial Government, recognition in which the British government followed suit by creating her a CBE in 1948. More accolades came in 1961, when she was elected a Fellow of the British Academy and was invited by the BBC to give the Reith Lectures. She was the first President of the African Studies Association of the UK. No less than five honorary degrees were conferred, including a Litt. D. from Cambridge. In 1965 she was created a Dame. This honour, signal in itself, was rendered even more so by the unusual – and in her case felicitous – decision to place the award not in the commoner Order of the British Empire but in the order of St Michael and St George, that predominantly Colonial Service order of chivalry. Her statutory retirement from the university in 1963 was more of a formality than an event. Indeed, at the age of eighty-four, Margery Perham sent off to her publishers the completed manuscript of her Nigerian diary of 1931, more than forty years (and a dozen books) after her first academic book and over fifty (years and articles) beyond her first publication.[3]

To complete the scenario, a brief explanation of the colonial policy of indirect rule is necessary. For it was Margery Perham's analysis and advocacy of indirect rule which was to represent her profoundest influence on the official mind of imperialism and of imperialists in action in Africa.

Lugard's own definition will serve as a start:

> The cardinal principle upon which the administration of N. Nigeria was based was what has been commonly called Indirect Rule, viz., rule through the Native Chiefs, who are regarded as an integral part of the machinery of Government, with well-defined powers and functions recognised by Government and by law, and not dependent on the caprice of an Executive Officer.[4]

Such chiefs were to be 'supported in every way and their authority upheld'. In an early interpretation of indirect rule Margery Perham described it as 'the characteristically British reaction to the political problem of Africa deriving partly from our conservatism, with its sense of historical continuity and its aristocratic tradition'.[5] Elsewhere she defined it as 'a system by which the tutelary power recognises existing African societies and assists them to adapt themselves to the functions of local government'.[6] Like her mentors, Lugard and Cameron, at the end of her career Margery Perham still challenged that

> critics should be asked what better method should have been applied at a time when the great majority of African tribes still maintained much of their rituality and separation.... Administrative Officers, with ever-growing duties and constant changes of posting, had to work to some accepted pattern.[7]

For her, 'to conserve the authority of traditional and established rulers wherever possible has been one of the principal axioms of British policy in Asia and Africa alike'.[8] That was what indirect rule was all about.

How did Margery Perham exercise her Oxford-based influence on those responsible for colonial administration? These included the policy-makers, whether at Westminster, in the Colonial Office, or in Government

House, and those who were responsible for putting policy into practice, the grass-roots colonial administrators. Her influence and her unambiguous association with the doctrine of indirect rule were put across in numerous ways, in her writings — books, articles, contributions to *The Times*, even two novels — and broadcasting, her committee work and teaching, her travels and personal encounters.

The most eloquent testimony to her contribution to and influence on colonial administration is to be found in her first scholarly book, *Native Administration in Nigeria* (1937). It was, at least until the publication of her biography of Lugard a quarter of a century later, the book by which Margery Perham was best known. Its value as a skilful interpretation of the principles of native administration in action, set within the very homeland of indirect rule, remains unimpaired today. What it has lost as a contribution to the study of the politics of Africa, it has gained as a prescribed text for the historical study of imperialism *in situ*. Not only did Margery Perham minutely describe the post-Lugardian scene; she was also able to compare the initial impact of Cameron's policy of 'indirect administration' with its antecedent 'indirect rule', and to anticipate how the aim of the development of native society and the growth of an educated élite might be accommodated within the parameters of indirect rule. Her own definition of indirect rule as 'the political education of the people'[9] parallels the basis of the Colonial Office's belief ten years later that

> the key to success lies in the development of an efficient democratic system of local government . . . which must not only find a place for the growing class of educated men but at the same time command the respect and support of the mass of the people.[10]

If criticism can be levelled, it is in three areas where, up to 1939, few students of the colonial scene in Africa, be they proconsuls, professors, or pressure groups, could yet provide a convincing answer. The first was the eventual shape of indirect rule. Understandably, Lugard was not concerned with defining its final goal at the very moment he was establishing its founding principles, but it could be deduced — and it was the assumption made by Margery Perham too — that the final outcome might lie in some kind of federation of native authorities, initially loose and largely financial. The second was the common misunderstanding of the educated élite and the 'problem of government' which they created. Margery Perham still saw their 'best' opportunities to lie in service with their native authorities. While their political ambitions were nomination to the Legislative Council, these should be met, not by giving them greater power over the more backward masses, but by increasing their responsibilities in Lagos colony and the urban centres. Somehow, Margery Perham believed, the emirate native authorities would remain as different as they had always been from the petty native administrations of the south. Finally, like practically every other observer of the period, Margery Perham's view of African nationalism was conditioned by the ubiquitous belief of 'indefinite time ahead', that Britain (and the world) had plenty of time to get the colonial problem right, for the day of Nigerian unity and hence independence was 'very distant'. How far her final judgement has been vindicated is a matter of personal assessment — '[Africa] is not a very ready soil for unity or democracy'[11] — but nothing can diminish the fact that here is a sophisticated, significant, and still important analysis of African colonial policy in practice at the high noon of empire and in its most notable territory. *Native Administration in Nigeria* remains a classic text in the literature on colonial administration, amply fulfilling her hopes of 'clothing the skeleton of the administrative system with flesh and blood'.[12]

Margery Perham was not to return exclusively to the principles of indirect rule in any other book: among her subsequent writing, Kenya, no admirer of indirect rule as a system of native administration, seems to have vied with Nigeria in her affections,[13] representing what Kenneth Robinson and Frederick Madden saw as 'the lion's share of her own work ... to which her interests most constantly returned'.[14] Nevertheless many of her books displayed her continuing fascination with indirect rule. Thus, in her life of Lugard (1960) she not only devoted two chapters to 'Indirect Rule, The Idea and The Structure', but a further fifty pages to a region-by-region analysis of its implementation,[15] and in *The Colonial Reckoning* (1963) she could not miss the opportunity to look back on Britain's half-century of colonial administration in Africa and set the system squarely in its context. 'Indirect Rule certainly had its merits,' she wrote. 'It broke the shock of Western annexation; it was economical; it held the peace; and it induced a sympathetic, enquiring attitude in colonial officials towards African society.'[16]

While we are discussing here only those of Margery Perham's books which had an influence on indirect rule, mention must be made of two particular genres of her literary contribution in book form. Both are essentially autobiographical in concept and content. These are her volumes entitled *Colonial Sequence* (1967, 1970) and her two (a third is in hand) 'diary' books, *African Apprenticeship* (1974) and *East African Journey* (1976). They throw as much light on colonial administration and on each territorial ethos of administration as on the indefatigable Margery Perham herself. *Colonial Sequence* consists of an extensive collection of her other writings: letters to *The Times*, talks in the *Listener*, articles by the score and introductions by the dozen, published during forty years of active interest and involvement in colonial policy. As an example of Margery Perham's influence on colonial affairs, in Britain and in the empire, this public testimony is likely to be surpassed only by her private correspondence with those who made and implemented that policy.

Writing introductions allowed her further to expand her views on matters which lay close to her heart. In her substantial introduction to K.D.D. Henderson's memorial to the life of that outstanding member of the Sudan Political Service, Sir Douglas Newbold, a tribute which together they accurately labelled *The Making of the Modern Sudan* (1953), she was able to present her views at length on the Sudan's temporary flirtation with indirect rule under the governorship of Sir John Maffey.[17] Newbold's correspondence, round which Henderson's biographical study is constructed, reveals the kind of close friendship which Margery Perham developed with a number of proconsuls. In such a context, it need be but a short step from personal friendship to policy influence, however subtle or sincere the process. In a shorter introduction to Robert Heussler's study of Sir Ralph Furse as the maker of the modern Colonial Service, *Yesterday's Rulers* (1963), she found considerable pleasure in thinking back over the era of Oxford's — and in particular her own — conspicuous role in training colonial administrators. In 1965 two attractive opportunities came along for Margery Perham to put forward once more her opinions on the place of indirect rule in the historiography of colonial administration in Africa. One was the invitation to contribute an introduction to a reprint of Lugard's classic treatise on colonial policy, *The Dual Mandate* (1922). Margery Perham, never one to do less than justice to publishers in such a context, produced an introduction of 10,000 words. The second came when she agreed to contribute a foreward to the present writer's *Principles of Native Administration in Nigeria, 1900–1947* (1965). Both books were central to an attractive blend of her dominant interests in British colonial administration: Lugard, Nigeria, indirect rule, and the grass-roots work of the District Officer.

Finally, there is the influential role in colonial studies played by Margery Perham in two series which she edited, 'The Economics of a

Tropical Dependency', in which Forde and Scott's *The Native Economies of Nigeria* appeared in 1946, and, two years later, *Mining, Commerce and Finance in Nigeria* by Bower *et al.*; and 'Studies in Colonial Legislatures', which started with Martin Wight's *The Development of the Legislative Council* (1946) and reached its sixth volume by 1952. She also edited several volumes in a 'Colonial and Comparative Studies' series between 1951 and 1959, besides editing reading lists in *Colonial Administration* (1946) and *Colonial Law* (1948).

Among her many articles in the professional journals, three stand out for their importance and influence on colonial administration. These are 'Native Administration in Tanganyika', which appeared in *Africa* in 1931; and the two major statements of 1934, 'Some Problems of Indirect Rule in Africa' (*Journal of the Royal Society of Arts*) and 'A Restatement of Indirect Rule' (*Africa*). Together with her *Native Administration in Nigeria* and the second volume of her life of Lugard, these form the essential corpus of her thought on the motivation, justification, and achievements of Britain's colonial trusteeship of the Africans. In them all, the moral message is loud and clear: Britain's empire must be motivated by 'the challenging ideal of philanthropy [which] saw the interests of the ruled as equal, if not superior, to those of their rulers'.[18]

Margery Perham's almost possessive use of *The Times* displays a singular exploitation of that newspaper's undisputed role as a vehicle for influence. Letters, leaders, articles, and obituaries, few aspects of *The Times* were overlooked in her campaign to influence opinion on colonial administration among those whose opinion was influential. We find this female 'Thunderer' starting her serious writing with two articles and a *Times* leader − no less! − in 1930. Such contributions were approaching the hundred mark by 1969, with letters progressively taking precedence over articles and leaders. By contrast she seems rarely to have reviewed books for *The Times* or elsewhere.

We have not yet finished with Margery Perham's use of the printed word as a tool for the projection of her views on the colonial condition and its particular aspect of colonial administration. It came as something of a surprise when, in her latter days, she admitted to the parentage of two novels, written more than fifty years before. The existence of these had been consistently omitted from bibliographies of her writings on colonial affairs: one of the first public listings, that published in connection with the *Festschrift* volume edited by her Oxford colleagues, coyly encloses one novel in square brackets, implying something that one does not really like to talk about in academic circles. Indeed, it was not until *Major Dane's Garden* was reprinted in 1970 that the semi-secret became public knowledge. It was written in 1922 soon after she had returned from a long recuperative visit to her sister Ethel Rayne (to whom, like the two-volume life of Lugard, it is dedicated):

> Though I was on the edge of an academic career, there was no one to tell me how to use my knowledge, such as it was, of the nature and problems of Somaliland. There was no routine of the D.Phil. in those days. So, needing an outlet for my deeply felt impression, I wrote a novel.

Leaving aside the inevitable datedness of much of its idiom,[19] the story does contain a number of insights into grass-roots colonial adminis-tration. Furthermore, in absolute terms it bears a certain badge of courage, for few white women had lived in Somaliland at that time and fewer still written about colonial service there. Little wonder that in the 1920s reviewers could innocently refer to M. Perham as *Mr* Per-ham![20] *Major Dane's Garden* retains a cachet of its own, as the first manifestation of what was to become Margery Perham's fifty-year love-affair with Africa.

Margery Perham was too astute a promoter of her own principles of colonial administration not to perceive the opportunity for the wider propagation of her faith opened up by the development of radio. She showed herself a determined performer. As early as 1934 she was broadcasting on the future relations between black and white in Africa. In the 1940s she went on the air quite regularly, talking about the colonial dilemma. Her triumph was to lie in the invitation to give the Reith Lectures. Significantly, she chose the theme 'The Colonial Reckoning'. For the first time she assumed the role of popularizer of what had been her somewhat eclectic views on British imperialism: now she became the man-in-the-street's interpreter of colonial admin-istration in addition to having been the *guru* of colonial administrators. This radio highlight was followed by an autobiographical series of talks, 'The Time of My Life'.

At the age of seventy-three Margery Perham courageously accepted an official invitation to fly out to Lagos to see for herself what the Nigerian civil war was all about. The Federal Military Government was worried that such an authoritative voice on Nigeria should be publicly adopting a pro-Biafran stance. She broadcast an open appeal to Colonel Ojukwu, the rebel leader, urging him that enough was enough. This she followed with an open letter in *The Times*, calling on him to surrender: 'Is it not better for the Biafrans to live not to fight but to work and flourish another day?'[21] Never one to lack moral courage, such a public 'conversion' must have cost her a lot. As a hostile letter to the pro-Ojukwu *Spectator* put it: 'If Dame Margery Perham is pro-Biafra, an anti-Biafran defies imagination.'[22]

Margery Perham's standing made her an obvious choice for committees concerned with colonial policy. We find her at an early age being retained as a consultant and commissioned, along with Oldham, Curtis, and Coupland, to put together a basic bibliography for the initiation of the Asian panjandrum Lord Hailey into the mysteries of Africa: 'Eating out of gold plate at Blicking Hall [Lothian's place], with Holbeins and Van Dycks softly lighted on the walls behind us, we planned the massive attack upon Africa South of the Sahara.' Her counsel was sought on the education of the young Kabaka.[23] Of her influential role in the shaping of the post-war programme for the training of colonial administrators at Oxford and of her persuasion of Sir Ralph Furse that hers were the better ideas, we have a good account in Robert Heussler's *Yesterday's Rulers* (1963). Her forthright arguments against the admission of Africans into the Administrative Service played a major part in influencing the Colonial Office to support what came to be known as the 'scaffolding policy', a hardening of the colonial heart against the training of Africans as future District Officers which even the animadversions of the mighty Hailey could not unfreeze.[24] She was a member of the Advisory Committee on Education in the Colonies from 1939 to 1945; of the 1944 Higher Education Commission and West Indies Higher Education Committee; and of the Executive Committee of Inter-University Council on Higher Education Overseas from 1946 to 1967. At Oxford we find her on the university's Committee for Colonial Studies and an occasional speaker at the Ralegh Club, to which she first gave a paper in 1933 (on, needless to say, 'Native Administration and Indirect Rule') but in which even she could not break the male domination of ordinary membership. We see her as a powerful figure in the Colonial Social Science Research Council and as a prime mover in the setting up of the Colonial Records Project. Those who recall her frequent appearances as a speaker at the post-war series of annual Colonial Office (later Cambridge) Summer Schools on African Administration may also remember she was the Vice-Chairman of Oxford's two pre-war Summer Conferences on Colonial Administration. All these ventures constituted a masterpiece in the manipulation of official opinion.

But of course, Margery Perham was above all — and throughout all —

a don at Oxford. In accordance with academic convention, these intellectual outlets (books, articles, broadcasts, committees) were part and parcel of her interpretation of the proper responsibilities of a university teaching post. 'From the base of my university', she once said, 'I have been travelling in the empire for about thirty years as a student of colonial government and of race relations.' So closely can these activities be interwoven that it is not always easy to identify which is the chicken and which the egg. In Margery Perham's case, if it was her base at Oxford which enabled her to build up her reputation as an authority on British colonial policy in Africa, it was her teaching of the Colonial Administrative Service (subsequently Devonshire) Courses at Oxford which put the seal on her standing within the Service as the authority on British colonial administration.

I suspect that, for many years at least, her teaching of administration to those future District Commissioners on the Oxford courses meant not so much public administration as native administration, and that native administration was more often than not synonymous with indirect rule. What I know, however, from personal experience in Africa is that indirect rule came to mean Margery Perham. It was commonplace when meeting Colonial Service colleagues in the 1950s for them to ask 'And how is Margery Perham?' After a recent radio talk about the Colonial Service, I received a letter from a former District Commissioner, who concluded: 'Do you see much of Margery Perham these days? *There's* someone who should have been a colonial governor!'

Two more aspects of her influence at Oxford are germane. One is the roll-call of pupils, many of them among the pioneer generation of African graduate students, whose theses on colonial government she supervised: their subsequent careers as well as their published works are acknowledgment enough. Even if Margery Perham could not rival Jowett, who could point to three of his pupils among the Viceroys of India, her friendship with countless colonial governors and African cabinet ministers enabled her to exert a similar influence. The other is the prominent capacity Margery Perham displayed for friendship, deep and lasting, both with her students at Oxford and with African leaders. Her relationship with Tom Mboya, at Ruskin and beyond, is a notable case in point; so, too, was her subsequent friendship with Yakubu Gowon.

Such a reputation as Great Britain's foremost academic expert on African administration was certainly not acquired by Margery Perham confining herself to seminars and Senior Common Rooms, or even by regular journeys to Downing or Great Smith Street. She was as well-known

a figure in Africa as she was in Oxford. Nor, like a certain class of
visitor instantly recognizable to Africa's men-on-the-spot, was she content to settle down in the cosseted luxury of Government House and, as
the saying was in Nigeria, 'never set foot beyond Carter Bridge'. Open
any page of the journal of her travels all over Africa, and you will find
her riding out to villages before breakfast, eating sandwiches on the
roadside, storming reluctant government offices; above all, keeping her
host up (Governor and District Officer alike) long after dinner with
searching questions on some aspect of colonial administration.

> After dinner, his wife having retired and Captain Hopkins, having
> learned with long practice to sleep with the inconspicuousness
> necessary to an ADC, the Governor and I talked. I count those long
> nightly talks with him as one of the most interesting events of my
> [East African] journey.

Or, 'I worked at the Residency until dinner *à deux* with my host. My
note-books are filling up rapidly.'[25] In Nigeria it was the same. 'Before
I settled into the Rest House, I called on the District Officer and persuaded him to take me out to see the market, the prison and the mission
before dark,' and, 'Here I am writing, sitting in the Governor's chair at
the Governor's table, and with the arms of England emblazoned above
my head.' Again, in Southern Rhodesia,

> I sat next to H.E. at dinner and drew him a bit. . . . Next day,
> Sunday, I worked hard, and in the evening went to talk with [the
> Chief Native Commissioner]. We engaged in deep and fascinating
> conversation . . . then I had an interview with the Governor. He was
> much better in his office than in his house and we had a very inter-
> esting talk. . . . On Rhodesia, unfortunately, he said little that was
> memorable.

Only a few District Officers used the forewarning gubernatorial
telegram to set out at once on an evasive prolonged safari. In Nigeria,
where colonial service was very much a man's life, Margery Perham
surprised a drunken District Officer, who greeted her arrival ahead of
schedule with 'Oh my God! Why did you come today? We thought you
would be quite impossible, so we drowned our sorrows *today*.' Few
academics in the 1930s, and likely no other woman (not even her
several sisters-in-arms in that 'upsurge of femininity in African studies'),
had anything to equal Margery Perham's experience of seeing for herself

what colonial administration was like on the ground.[26] None achieved
quite the same wide sense of respect and rapport, almost reverence,
among the men-on-the-spot. Here, perhaps, lay Margery Perham's secret:
the strength of her position as an authority on colonial administration
rested on the fact that she met and knew (and often had taught) the
African administrators in the field. Her writing and her teaching, then,
bore the hallmark *of* the professional – *for* the professionals.

Let me conclude this section with two incidents in Margery Perham's
African travels which do not feature in her own travelogues. In 1958,
no longer titupping in the saddle but still penetrating up-country,
Margery Perham arrived at Zaria, in northern Nigeria. If she was going
to be expected to teach African administrative officers at Oxford (as
was now becoming the case), she intended to see for herself how they
were – or were not – being trained in their own country. At the end
of her visitation she conceded that our non-graduate cadets were better
than the graduate ADOs to whom she had been entrusted as escorts –
'at least your chaps can perform out in the districts, where real administration lies, and don't prefer to sit around in HQ.' The other incident
reveals Margery Perham in a characteristically fearless mood. During her
official visit to Nigeria at the height of the civil war, she met at the
front Brigadier Adekunle, the fiery commander of the 3rd Infantry
Brigade justifiably known as 'The Black Scorpion'. He tried to brow-
beat her and order her around. Her reaction was short and sharp: 'Young
man,' she said to the admittedly youthful Brigadier, 'you had better
pray I never have you in my seminar at Oxford.'

This prime ability to meet and talk on equal terms with the man-on-
the-spot (colonial governor, District Officer, emir or native administration official) and to gain his confidence was a researcher's advantage
which Margery Perham pursued with equal vigour, and comparable
success, back in the metropolis.

In retrospect it appears that, while in the 1920s Margery Perham was
building up a corpus of knowledge from her role as confidante of
governors, officials, and ministers, in the 1940s and 1950s she spread
her influence down to the middle (District Officer) and lower (pro-
bationer) ranks of the Colonial Service by philosophizing to them
at Oxford from the facts and ideas she had pieced together during the
1930s. Of course, the men-on-the-spot may well have influenced Margery
Perham as much as she influenced them. Nor should one be misled into
thinking of Margery Perham as every field administrator's cup of tea.
We know that, in the essentially male world of colonial administration,
she did not bring unqualified joy to the heart of every bachelor

administrator in bush and boma, least of all when she was known to be coming hotfoot from Government House. There is evidence, too, to suggest her visits to Africa were less than welcome to some governors (for example, Grigg in Kenya) and that in the Colonial Office by the 1950s her name could, like Lugard's half a century earlier, rouse the spectre of 'Oh no, not again'. I should be surprised if her personal correspondence does not include an exchange of letters with all the leading figures in colonial policy-making of the day.[27] A unique opportunity to exploit this came through her close friendship with Lord Lugard. Those involved in colonial policy who made the pilgrimage to Abinger to consult the original oracle very often met an up-and-coming neophyte, too, namely Margery Perham.[28] It would be intellectually unfair, and also chronologically inaccurate, to attribute to Margery Perham, as some of her critics have done, the image of Lugard as a proconsular giant. He had already proved that role for himself, in a number of eminent capacities and helped by Flora Shaw's unflagging canvassing of his name, long before Margery Perham was ever introduced to him. What she may justifiably be guilty of, if that is the right word, is the enmythification of Lugard as the perfect and peerless proconsul. Certainly her contiguity with him and his confidence in her proved to be mutually enriching. This in turn led to her involvement with the colonial establishment, first in the preparatory work at the Royal Institute of International Affairs for Hailey's *An African Survey* (1938), and later in Colonial Office committees.

If we are to base our assessment of the influence Margery Perham exercised on her writings, we must accept that, while some like Kenneth Robinson and Frederick Madden honoured her with a *Festschrift*, others were much more critical of her work. This counter-image is at its most prominent in the writing of D.J.M. Muffett, in his attack on Lugard's record as High Commissioner in Northern Nigeria in *Concerning Brave Captains* (1964), and in the iconoclasm of I.F. Nicolson, first in his account of Lugard's deliberate misunderstanding of the quality of the Southern administration, and, more vigorously yet, in the damning exposure of Lugard's opportunism and his wife's scheming, in *The Administration of Nigeria: Men, Methods and Myths* (1969) — with its puzzling postscript 'Dame Margery Perham's Writings on Nigeria'. True or false, these are reflections of an influence which the would-be biographer must take into consideration. Incidentally, although no biography of Margery Perham has yet been written, she is, unusually, the subject of a Ph.D. thesis — in Norwegian.

This chapter is seeking to convey an impression of the remarkable influence of one woman on the overwhelmingly male preserve of colonial administration. If this influence needs spelling out today, it was a fact of life which up to the end of the empire was never in doubt among the politicians and the practitioners, among the professionals themselves: Margery Perham's name had become too intimately linked with that of colonial administration and indirect rule for it to be otherwise. I have shown some of the ways in which that influence upon colonial policies was exercised: by writing and broadcasting, by committees and travelling, by listening to the men-on-the-spot, and by teaching generations of future men-on-the-spot.[29] For many a Colonial Service officer and Colonial Office official, Margery Perham was *the* African expert. 'Her name spells Africa,' declared Kenneth Robinson and Frederick Madden on her retirement from Oxford.[30] In the nature of academic evaluation, time may alter the estimate of her successors. It may suggest that she changed less quickly than she ought when those in charge changed, and that her own influence declined with the passing of that empire after the mid-1960s, above all with the ending of the Devonshire Courses at Oxford and the closing of the Colonial Office in 1966. Yet nothing can alter the esteem in which by and large colonial officialdom held her. Complex as the strands of this reputation were, the formula itself is simple. Margery Perham advanced from being in the 1930s, when in Madden's words she had 'a whole continent almost to herself',[31] the expert on indirect rule as a policy of colonial administration, through her influence on the colonial administrators whom she taught at Oxford in the 1940s and 1950s, to her role in 1960 as the biographer of Lugard and the doyenne of the new field of 'African Studies'. The circle was complete. It was Lugard who had translated the theory of indirect rule into the practice of native administration, who had built his practical *Political Memoranda* into his theoretical *Dual Mandate*. With both indirect rule and native administration, the name of Lugard was inseparable. Now the name of Margery Perham became inseparable from both Lugard and colonial administration. Finally, because Margery Perham was throughout these influential years of 1924 to 1963 a don at Oxford, the policy and principles of indirect rule, native administration, and colonial administration all became linked with the name of Oxford. We can no more separate Lugard from indirect rule or Margery Perham from both and from Oxford, than we can separate Gilbert from Sullivan or Robinson from Gallagher. In the words of Kenneth Robinson and Frederick Madden, 'If Margery Perham's name spells Africa, it is also especially connected with Oxford.'

Nevertheless, three caveats must be entered in this attribution to Margery Perham of an Oxford influence on colonial administration, with particular reference to the image of any Oxford School of indirect rule. First, when we talk of Margery Perham and Oxford, her influence was predominantly exercised not on the views of the thousands of run-of-the-mill undergraduates each year (the essential 'Oxford'), but principally on the two or three dozen Colonial Service probationers who attended the annual Course 'A' (later this included a handful of senior men returning from the field for Course 'B'); those attending the two Oxford University Summer Schools on Colonial Administration; and, most recently, postgraduate students, African and American as well as British, reading for a higher degree in colonial government or modern African history. This influence could be extended to Cambridge (where, because of a shortage of expertise in the field of government, she had to lecture to their Colonial Services courses, too!)[32] and later to London probationers, for her works on colonial administration became recommended texts to be read along with *The Dual Mandate* and *An African Survey*. The Margery Perham/Oxford influence was as wide outside Oxford as inside.

Secondly, it would be wrong to set up the false antithesis of 'Oxford and indirect rule' opposed by 'Cambridge and local government'. The temptation exists, for the final — and successful — assault on indirect rule and its replacement by local government as a principle of colonial administration was launched from a positively identifiable Cambridge base. Andrew Cohen and Ronald Robinson, in the vanguard of the movement to kill off indirect rule, were both Cambridge men. They not only pressed into their service the new African Studies Branch of the Colonial Office and its *Journal of African Administration*, but were also able to manipulate the agenda and attendance at the Colonial Office (later Cambridge) Summer Schools on African Administration, especially the critical ones between 1947 and 1951, so as to bury the ghost of indirect rule once and for all. Hence the change of policy in the Colonial Office, encapsulated in the Local Government Despatch of 1947, where Creech Jones's key concepts of 'efficient, representative and local' were tantamount to the sounding of the death-knell for indirect rule.[33] Its final epitaph was written by Ronald Robinson in a now famous article.[34] But to argue that, because local government had supplanted indirect rule, Cambridge had thus won out over Oxford in the teaching of colonial administration is too naïve. Two of the most outspoken and influential critics of indirect rule were Oxford men. W.R. Crocker (who had impressed Margery Perham as having the best mind in Nigeria, excluding only the Governor, Sir Donald Cameron) published in 1936 a devastating critique of British colonial adminis- tration. He dismissed 'the elaborate façade' of indirect rule as 'much ado about nothing – cardboard and plaster patched up by the careerists', warning that 'no more damning remark could be made in the annual report on an officer than that he was "direct" or was not sufficiently imbued with the spirit of indirect rule'.[35] A second major critic of indirect rule, and the most awesome of them all, was Lord Hailey, eminent among Oxford's proconsular alumni. Hailey considered the term indirect rule 'lacking in precision'. What it stood for he did not like: 'The principle of Indirect Rule has passed through the stages of first, a useful administrative device, then of a political doctrine, and finally that of a religious dogma.'[36] He had little faith in the kind of local administration often thrown up by indirect rule outside the Nigerian emirates, which he caricatured as 'a mass moot of clan elders [whose] influence was acquired by the practice of wizards'.[37] Yet, if Cambridge could not equal either the contempt of Oxford men in their vilification of indirect rule or their ardour in its implication, at least the gubernatorial enthusiasts for indirect rule came from both universities. Charles Temple, William Gowers, and Shenton Thomas were Cambridge men; Richmond Palmer and John Maffey were from Oxford. Lugard, and Cameron, the two supreme architects of indirect rule, went to neither university.

The third caveat is that, for all the undoubted influence of Margery Perham's 'Devonshire' kingdom, that was not the only institution at Oxford where indirect rule was projected. The role of the Institute of Social Anthropology under E. Evans-Pritchard, and particularly the research of many of its staff members, calls for closer examination in the context of Oxford and colonial administration. This could be a useful extension of the continuing debate on the exact nature of the relationship between anthropology and colonial administration, variously viewed as helpmate, handmaiden, and harlot.

The name of Margery Perham is rightly associated with indirect rule and native administration. Yet no one could have been more careful, from the very beginning, to point to the defects of indirect rule as well as its merits. As early as 1934 she warned that indirect rule must not be static: 'The immediate test of its success will be the frequency with which it receives and requires revision in response to progress.'[38] Later, she identified an inherent defect in it.[39] It was, like so much the British carried abroad with them, an almost wholly political concept. The colonial governors, still following *laissez-faire* in economics, let loose large economic forces which weakened or even destroyed the tribal structures upon which the new system had to be built. 'Indirect Rule' required 'several quiet generations' – which two world wars and an economic slump made sure it never got.[40] Towards the end of her teaching career, Margery Perham was still arguing, alongside the merits of indirect rule, that 'too much success can crystallise administration. . . . While at best the system [of indirect rule] could and did reform and modernise native societies, at worst it could stereotype them.'[41] Finally, after her retirement, she reflected that

> I think I can claim to have recognised that the Indirect Rule principle was not universally applicable. To the surprise both of the Colonial Service and the majority of the Africans themselves, the outer world, with its powerful economic forces and political ideas, broke in upon Africa's long isolated world, so that rapid adjustments were needed. . . . It was of course easier for the travelling critic to recognise these forces than it was for a Service, scattered about Africa, more of its members in the bush than in the few towns or among the tribes most exposed to the new forces.[42]

In the 1930s as in the 1960s Margery Perham's message on indirect rule was unambiguous: 'I seem to have dealt almost exclusively with its defects and difficulties. I have done so because I realise that in complacency lies its greatest danger.'[43] In the promotion of indirect rule she was less its preacher than its teacher. Indirect rule, fashioned by Lugard in Nigeria, received official endorsement from the Colonial Office Conference of 1930. For all her enthusiasm, it always remained a Colonial Office policy – never an Oxford ploy or a Perham plaything.

We are left with a final question. What was the mainspring of Margery Perham's tireless and sincere commitment to indirect rule and to Africa? Friend and confidante of those responsible for colonial policy, she was herself no colonial administrator. The answer would seem to lie in her feeling of the need for an unbreachable moral imperative in Britain's imperial 'trusteeship'. She would have approved of A.P. Thornton's vision of the role of the British empire as 'to bring light to dark places, to teach the true political method . . . to act as trustee for the weak . . . and to represent in itself the highest aims of human society'.[44] In a series of characteristically forthright articles to *The Times* in 1936[45] she underlined how this concept of trusteeship had been devalued by its transfer to the sphere of geo-politics and recalled its basic meaning of 'unqualified service to the interests of our wards', arguing that this kind of trusteeship, 'the training of subject peoples in self-government', should be the mainspring of our colonial policy. Once this strict sense of morality is grasped, its presence behind the consistent advocacy of indirect rule as the 'best' system of native administration immediately becomes distinguishable. Britain's twentieth-century role in Africa for Margery Perham still retained the nineteenth-century legacy of some kind of civilizing mission:

> For myself and the few others of my generation in the 1920s and 1930s this light had not yet begun to shine. Away from the Western bulge and a very few lucent regions in the middle and the East, tropical Africa remained dark, if not quite 'darkest'.[46]

Hence, too, her deep admiration of the whole anti-slavery movement and the Aborigines' Protection Society, as revealed in her Reith Lectures. The humanitarian link with the nineteenth century meant a lot to her, and great was her pleasure when, through her friendship with Lugard, she was 'helped in vivid fashion to conjure up the Africa of the 1880s and to hear him talk of his friend Sir John Kirk, fellow-explorer with Livingstone in the 1850s'. The message of morality and mutual respect stood forth in the very first introduction she ever wrote:

> In many parts of Africa we see a clumsy dictation in place of the experiments in partnership which are open to us. . . . It is possible to work in a spirit of high altruism *for* 'natives'; it seems more natural, on the other hand, to work *with* 'individuals.' Their wishes and feelings begin to come into the picture as well as our standards of what is right and efficient.[47]

Such a high level of morality was as evident in her private life as it was in public word and action. She was for many years a devoted member of North Oxford's well-known Church of St Philip and St James; and inadvertently to invite her to dinner in Lent or to forget her vegetarian principles in other seasons (on moral, not dietary grounds: witness her vigorous campaign against battery hens), were pitfalls to avoid. Consider, too, her own family. Her father was a keen churchman. An adherent of the Oxford movement, he sent his children to positively Christian boarding-schools. At St Anne's, Abbots Bromley, the young Margery Perham found the headmistress 'a stately, splendidly aristo-cratic, devout and authoritarian woman'. Margery Perham's uncle was a missionary in Malaya, where he translated the prayer-book into Dayak and ended up as Archdeacon of Singapore. Her beloved sister Ethel set sail for East Africa in 1910 intending to take up missionary work, but by the time she landed she was engaged and was married in Mombasa Cathedral. Each time Margery Perham returned from a visit to Africa, she came back inspired by 'the spirit of devotion' displayed by District Officers and convinced that the faith the Christian missionaries gave to African peoples was perhaps 'most precious of all'.

From beginning to end her work in and writing on Africa was shot through with the same belief: the line she drew under the colonial account in her last book, in 1963, was the same as the conclusion of her first, a quarter-century earlier: 'The tutelage of Africans by humane and experienced nations is the only means of applying that training for organising and maintaining an independent and democratic state system in the modern world.'[48] As Kenneth Robinson and Frederick Madden summed up on Margery Perham's retirement, she brought, perhaps predominantly, a profound and continued preoccupation with the moral issues in the exercise of imperial rule, sharpened by her own Christian conviction no less than her familiarity with the great debates of the nineteenth-century humanitarianism in Britain.[49]

Margery Perham, like Rhodes and Milner, Curzon and Hailey, is assured of a place among Oxford's imperial immortals. Not, as with them, as an empire-builder, but, along with Jowett, as the builder of empire-builders. For her, as for them, Oxford's unquestioned role in the preparation of Britain's proconsuls was the kind reflected in Cromer's lofty vision of a Sudan staffed by 'a cadre of active young men endowed with good health, high character and fair abilities . . . the flower of those who are turned out from our schools and colleges',[50] or that echoed in Kipling's arrogant imperative

> Take up the White Man's Burden,
> Send forth the best ye breed.

For Margery Perham, too, if those proconsuls-in-the-making thus sent forth by her could be weaned on the rusk of indirect rule, so much the better for ruled and ruler alike. As she once told a gathering of distinguished colonial administrators: 'In all circumstances Indirect Rule is more effective than Direct Rule as a political training for tribal officials. . . . So as not to leave a mistaken impression, I had better state my profound belief in it.'[51]

Thus spake *Africa ipsissima*.

Notes

1. The principal biographical sources from which the data in this chapter are drawn are, apart from personal information, Margery Perham's radio talk of 11 January 1972 in 'The Time of My Life' series; her presidential address to the inaugural meeting of the African Studies Association of the United Kingdom, held at the University of Birmingham in September 1964; and the introduction to her autobiographical *East African Journey* (1976). Unattributed quotations in the text derive from these three primary sources.

2. Major Henry R. Rayne, DSO, MC. He wrote two accounts of his work there, *Sun, Sand and Somalis* (1921), and *The Ivory Raiders* (1923).

3. This has not yet been published.

4. Sir Frederick Lugard, *Political Memoranda*, 1918 (1970), No. IX, para. 1.

5. Margery Perham, 'A Restatement of Indirect Rule', *Africa* (1934), p. 332.

6. Margery Perham, 'Some Problems of Indirect Rule in Africa', address to the Royal Society of Arts, 24 March 1934.

7. Margery Perham, *Colonial Sequence, I: 1930-1949* (1967), pp. xix, xviii.

8. *The Times* leader [Margery Perham] (27 November 1930).

9. Margery Perham, *Native Administration in Nigeria* (1937), p. 345.

10. Secretary of State's despatch on Local Government in the African Territories dated 25 February 1947, reprinted in A.H.M. Kirk-Greene, *The Principles of Native Administration in Nigeria, 1900-1947* (1965), pp. 238-48.

11. Perham, *Native Administration*, p. 362.

12. Perham, *Native Administration*, p. x. My own copy is valuably enhanced with *marginalia* from men in the field forty years ago. One of these, inscribed from a hospital bed at remote Azare in the year of publication, runs: 'I don't usually write in books, but as the medicine men have just removed my appendix I have a lot of time on my hands and will read anything.'

13. On my first field trip to Kenya, I sent a postcard to Margery Perham, saying 'Tell it not in Kano, publish it not in the streets of Zaria, . . . I have found God's answer to the African administrator's Paradise: send all the Hausa-Fulani to Kenya.'

14. Kenneth Robinson and Frederick Madden (eds.), *Essays in Imperial Government* (1963), p. vii.

15. Margery Perham, *Lugard: the Years of Authority* (1960), chapters 7, 8, and 22-4. To her chagrin, this was not to be the definitive life as it was then hailed: I.F. Nicolson, *The Administration of Nigeria: Men, Methods and Myths* (1969), and D.J. Muffett, *Concerning Brave Captains* (1964), saw to that, leaving J.E. Flint to do his best to reconcile a halo of perfection with feet of clay – see his essay on Lugard in L.H. Gann and Peter Duignan (eds.), *African Proconsuls* (1978), pp. 290-312.

16. Margery Perham, *The Colonial Reckoning* (1963), p. 58.

17. Of Maffey's wholesale introduction of indirect rule into the Sudan, Newbold recalled how the system had been 'rather run to death by romantic D.C.s, especially in Northern Nigeria, recreating little native states on a squire-archical basis' – quoted in K.D.D. Henderson, *The Making of the Modern Sudan* (1953), p. 531.

18. Perham, *Colonial Reckoning*, p. 103.

19. Favourite lines are legion, among them the too-good-to-be-true image of 'she was the sort of girl that all boys can like and all girls can love' and the today-sexist remark to the DC by the heroine, 'I don't see that it's a woman's business to worry about the principles of native government – I love you, and I'd defend your policy against the world'. Unsurprisingly, the *Philadelphia Public Ledger* heralded the book under the headline 'Honor Triumphs Over Sordid Passion'.

20. She wrote a second novel, *Josie Vine* (1927), and an unpublished play about Anglo-Saxon England.

21. *The Times* (9 September 1968). In private, Margery Perham confided to me that she would have been wiser to use the term 'negotiation' rather than 'surrender' in her broadcast.

22. 9 September 1968.

23. Richard Symonds kindly drew my attention to the correspondence between Makerere College and Margery Perham (1942) in the university archives.

24. Cf. Perham, *Native Administration*, p. 361, and Lord Hailey, *Native Administration and Political Development in British Tropical Africa* (1941, first public edition 1979), pp. 47-8.

25. All quotations in this paragraph are taken verbatim from her published Central (1974) and East (1976) African, and her unfinished West African, diaries.

26. In parenthesis, let us remember that field research was in one way much easier in the Africa of the 1930s than it is today. Under the umbrella of His Excellency and with District Officers requested to take her under their personal care, doors opened, meetings were arranged, and files made available to Margery Perham in a way that is the envy of the post-independence researcher in Africa.

27. I have not seen Margery Perham's personal correspondence with Sir Donald Cameron, but the warmth and respect of the letters written to her by Sir Douglas Newbold, the greatest of the Sudan's Civil Secretaries, and her friendship with Sir James Robertson, Newbold's successor and then the last of Nigeria's British Governors-General, reveal the quality of the terms on which she could meet colonial administrators. It was an experience in itself, at St Antony's in 1978, when we managed to muster, probably for the last time ever (a sort of museum-piece grand finale, I suppose) some seventy former colonial governors, PCs and DCs — and Lord Boyd to boot, the Service's favourite Secretary of State — to watch how they all wanted to talk again with Margery Perham and how much mutual pleasure this gave.

28. I recently learned much more about the Abinger Hammer visitors when I interviewed Miss Violet Townshend, Lugard's personal secretary — see A.H.M. Kirk-Greene, 'Amanuensis to Lord Lugard', *West Africa* (1979), pp. 157-9.

29. There was even a poem, in the *Spectator* (May 1936).

30. Robinson and Madden (eds.), *Essays*, p. vii.

31. In discussion at the Commonwealth history seminar, Nuffield College, June 1980.

32. Margery Perham's own recollections of the Colonial Service courses at Cambridge differ from mine as one of their members. 'I remember it well', she has recalled, 'because of the astonishing difference in the atmosphere of the two places which had already affected the two sets of officers — Oxford so hyper-sophisticated and blasé, Cambridge so young and keen and so polite they even laughed at the jokes which were received in silence at Oxford.'

33. 'It announced to the African governors that the old household gods of Indirect Rule had been cast out of the Colonial Office and directed them to do likewise.' Ronald Robinson in W.H. Morris-Jones and Georges Fischer (eds.), *Decolonisation and After* (1980), p. 64.

34. R.E. Robinson, 'Why "Indirect Rule" has been replaced by "Local Government" ', *Journal of African Administration* (July 1950), pp. 12-15.

35. W.R. Crocker, *Nigeria* (1936), pp. 222, 217.

36. Lord Hailey, 'Some problems dealt with in *An African Survey*', *International Affairs* (March 1939), p. 202.

37. Lord Hailey, *Native Administration in the British African Territories, III: West Africa* (1951), p. 97.

38. Perham, 'A Restatement', p. 334.

39. Margery Perham, 'African Pro-Consul' [Lugard], *Listener* (2 June 1965).

40. Ibid. Although in the Reith Lectures in 1961 Margery Perham could smile at the senior Colonial Office official who had said to her, in 1939, 'Well, at any rate in Africa we can be sure that we have unlimited time in which to work', she herself had written only two years before, about Nigeria, 'We have an interval within which to build up, as a foundation for unity and democracy, that wide and active citizenship which we neglected to prepare in India' (*Native Administration*, p. 360).

41. Perham, *Colonial Reckoning*, p. 58.

42. Perham, Introduction, *Colonial Sequence*, I, p. xix. In a memorable phrase, she dismissed the inflexible commitment of indirect rule to supporting the traditional chiefs against *vox populi*: 'It may look noble to put a king upon an ace but it does not take the trick' (*Colonial Reckoning*, p. 116).

43. Perham, 'Problems of Indirect Rule', p. 18.

44. A.P. Thornton, *The Imperial Idea and its Enemies* (1959), pp. ix–x.

45. *The Times* (10, 11, and 12 February 1936).

46. This and the following quotations are taken from her African Studies Association address, 1964.

47. Perham, Introduction, *Ten Africans* (1936), p. ii.

48. Perham, *Native Administration*, p. 362.

49. Robinson and Madden (eds.), *Essays*, p. vi.

50. Lord Cromer, *Political and Literary Essays* (1914), p. 4.

51. Perham, 'A Restatement', p. 334.

While the proofs for this book were being corrected, Dame Margery Perham died on 19 February 1982, aged 86.

　KEITH HANCOCK AND IMPERIAL ECONOMIC
HISTORY: A RETROSPECT FORTY YEARS ON

David Fieldhouse

When one sets out to assess the impact of a major historian on his field
of study there is an inevitable danger that his importance will be
exaggerated. Alexander Pope gave Newton perhaps the highest praise
ever accorded to a scholar in his famous couplet:

> Nature and Nature's Laws lay hid in Night:
> God said, Let Newton be! and all was Light.

I do not suggest that Hancock was the founder of serious study of the
economic history of modern colonialism, still less that he grasped and
solved all its riddles. Even the greatest historian has to build on what
he inherits and is circumscribed by the preoccupations and limited
vision of his own time. Moreover, Hancock did not carry on the very
fruitful investigation he worked out in the later 1930s. His major
contribution to the field consists of the two parts of the second volume
of his *Survey of British Commonwealth Affairs, Problems of Economic
Policy, 1918-1939*, which were published in 1940 and 1942, but had
almost been completed before September 1939. Thereafter he published
only two small books on or related to the subject: *Argument of Empire*
for Penguin in 1943, and *Wealth of Colonies*, given as the Marshall
Lectures in 1950 and published by the Cambridge University Press the
same year. These were afterthoughts. From 1942 most of his time was
spent on writing the official *British War Economy* (1949) and editing
the multi-volume *History of the Second World War*. Then he moved on
to his great project on Smuts, which, together with his commitment to
help found the Australian National University, absorbed most of his
energy until his retirement in the late 1960s. Thus, although he never
lost interest in the economics of imperialism and colonialism, he did
not find time to build on his original foundations; and this means that,
in assessing his influence on colonial economic history, one has to
concentrate primarily on the *Survey*, and to ask the fundamental
question whether these two books should now be regarded as a major
landmark and, if so, on what grounds. In attempting to answer it I
propose to start with a short account of some of the main literature

144

on imperial economic history as it existed in the middle — and late — 1930s to establish Hancock's intellectual inheritance; then to summarize the central arguments; and finally to relate his approach to that of economic historians in the following four decades.

Imperial Economic History before the later 1930s

In 1934 Hancock was appointed Professor of History at Birmingham University. He was thirty-six and had had a brilliant career as an undergraduate at Melbourne, assistant lecturer at Perth, Rhodes Scholar at Balliol, Fellow of All Souls, and Professor of History at Adelaide. (In 1944 he became Chichele Professor of Economic History and returned to All Souls, where he stayed until 1949 when he went to London, as Director of the newly established Institute of Commonwealth Studies in Russell Square.) He had so far published only two things of any significance on the Commonwealth: his now famous *Australia* (1930), and the chapter 'The Commonwealth [of Australia] 1900-1914' in volume VII, part 1, of the *Cambridge History of the British Empire (CHBE)* (1933). In fact, he was better known for his book on *Ricasoli and the Risorgimento in Tuscany* (1926). It was, presumably on the basis of his Australian publications, and certainly on the recommendation of Lionel Curtis, that Arnold Toynbee invited him in 1934 to write the first *Survey* in the new Commonwealth series projected by Chatham House;[1] and Hancock later wrote that he accepted because 'it would give me first-hand knowledge of a group of states living in tension between the dangerous pressures of external circumstances and their own domestic habits of law, liberty, persuasion and compromise'. His problem was to discover whether the Commonwealth could 'genuinely fulfil its profession and programme' and could 'make itself a spacious and free policy acceptable not only to Canadians, Australians and New Zealanders but also to Indians, Burmese and Africans — not to mention the Irish'.[2] That is to say, Hancock, like any historian embarking on what was to him a comparatively new field of study, had to establish his terms of reference. He had also to build on the existing stock of concepts and the published work; and one can imagine him during the next five years reading all there was, adding his own research, and eventually coming up with his own synthesis. What, then, was the historiography he inherited?

On the political and constitutional side, which he dealt with in volume I of the *Survey*, but with which I am not concerned here, there was a good deal, for the established tradition of imperial history was primarily constitutional. By the mid-1930s some substantial and enduring work had been published on colonial economics in continental America and the Caribbean before 1815, together with the first generation of more or less properly researched work on the settlement colonies of the nineteenth century. This traditional branch of imperial history had three main pillars: settlement and the problem of land policy; the development of viable export staples in the colonies; and the central role of Britain in providing a market, exports, and capital investment. In current thought all these pointed to the essential complementarity of the British and Dominion economies, which was supposed to have achieved expression in the Ottawa Conference and imperial preference in 1932. To a critical historian, however, this consensus provided a challenge: he must sort out the arguments for and against imperial economic integration, stimulated by the fact that by the later 1930s serious cracks were developing in the Ottawa system. In this field, at least, Hancock's intellectual inheritance was valuable.

On the rest of the empire, however, Hancock can have found much less guidance. It would be an exaggeration to say that there was no economic history of the modern British colonies by the mid-1930s, but there was little of real value. As I have said, there was a good deal on the first British empire, and from this body of material two obvious themes emerged – imperial monopoly versus free trade and slave versus free labour – and Hancock made full use of both. But what were the issues on which the economic history of the bulk of the modern dependent territories could be made to turn? Very little had been published on them by the 1930s and it is significant that the *CHBE* neither included a volume on these territories nor provided much information on them in the general volumes II and III, published respectively in 1940 and 1959. In planning part two of his *Problems of Economic Policy*, Hancock had two guides to the general issues: the first and third volumes of Lilian Knowles's *Economic Development of the Overseas Empire* (1924, 1936) and Allan McPhee's *The Economic Revolution in British West Africa* (1926). In addition there was a growing literature on the problems, particularly the moral problems, of labour supply in colonial Africa, notably R. Buell's *The Native Problem in Africa* (1928), M.R. Dilley's *British Policy in Kenya Colony* (1937), Margery Perham's *Native Administration in Nigeria* (1937), Lucy Mair's *Native Policies in Africa* (1936), and Lord Hailey's *An African Survey* (1938) which was also commissioned by Chatham House on the instigation of Curtis. Far more had been published on southern Africa than any other part of that continent, and this literature also concentrated primarily on problems of race. Among those books Hancock obviously used were W.M. Macmillan's *The South African Agrarian Problem and its Historical Development* (1919), E.H. Brookes's *The History of Native Policy in South Africa from 1830 to the Present Day* (1924) and *The Colour Problems of South Africa* (1934), S.H. Frankel's *Cooperation and Competition in the Marketing of Maize in South Africa* (1926), and Margery Perham and Lionel Curtis's *The Protectorates of South Africa, The Question of their Transfer to the Union* (1935).

These were all on British or other possessions in Africa. It is clear, however, that in formulating the issues he thought critical in tropical dependencies Hancock was heavily influenced by A. De. Kat Angelino's classic, *Colonial Policy* (1931), which made the Netherlands Indies everyone's model for assessing the merits of alternative economic and social policies in tropical colonies and which stimulated the later spate of books by Furnival, Vlekke, and others that were published in and after 1939. One other potentially valuable guide which Hancock had read was R.C. Dutt's *The Economic History of India in the Victorian Age* (1904) which, one would have thought, set out many of the fundamental issues involved in the economic relations between an imperial power and its dependencies. My impression, however, is that Hancock did not methodically relate the standard Indian complaints — about imposed free trade, monetary policy, and official preference for alien over indigenous sources for the supply of public stores — to other colonies: perhaps he, like so many others, thought of India in a different way from other colonies.[3]

What, then, was the guidance these and similar studies gave Hancock on the themes he should develop in his *Survey*? First, on South Africa, they suggested that there were two parallel issues: the attempt being made by whites to safeguard their standard of living and culture by segregation and job reservation; second, the policy of reserves for Africans which complemented segregation but also had humanitarian elements. In economic terms the problem Hancock set out to solve was how far these policies reflected economic realities and what the economic consequences were likely to be. Here at least possible lines of investigation seemed clearly established for him by the existing literature. It was, however, less clear what approach he should adopt to tropical dependencies. The literature divided into two categories, to some extent chronologically. In the 1920s the overriding preoccupation was still with what Chamberlain had called 'undeveloped estates' and Frenchmen such as Albert Sarraut the problem of 'la mise en valeur': the economic history of tropical Africa could be divided between an earlier period of self-sufficiency coupled with an external trade based on slavery in America and a modern era in which development flowed from 'legitimate trade', improved communications, and investment by Europeans. This was the central theme of McPhee's book on West Africa, itself an impressive pioneering work but which, because it was written before 1929, breathed an optimism in the potentialities of what has later been called the 'open economy' which could no longer be fully accepted by the time Hancock wrote.

In fact most work published on tropical economic development belonged to a second category which was started well before 1930 and whose dominant feature was doubt about both the economic and moral consequences of the traditional approach to development there. Lilian Knowles's long chapter in the 1924 volume I of her trilogy, 'Problems of the Tropics', pointed to fundamental moral and practical problems relating to employment, land, types of agricultural production (particularly peasant versus plantation methods), education, and taxation. She even briefly queried (following Lugard) how much the commodity trade in West Africa and elsewhere actually benefited the African producer. Buell in 1928 had highlighted the danger that African labour might be exploited even within a liberal economic and political system; and the South African authors demonstrated the monstrous effects land monopoly and segregation were having on African peasants. For Indonesia De Kat Angelino showed how peasants might be exploited under both 'liberal' and 'ethical' systems by merchants, planters, and the state. Thus, although for most of tropical Africa the evidence was still scanty, at least Hancock was bound to be aware that the assumption that unqualified benefits flowed from the incorporation of colonial societies into the international economy needed careful examination. I suspect that it was from Knowles above all that he inherited a promising conceptual framework: was a trading economy, even if run in line with the moral dictates of the 'trust' for 'backward' peoples, really in the best interests of the colonies and their inhabitants?

To summarize the state of the subject in the years after 1934, one could say that Hancock inherited three main issues: first, the viability of an imperial economy centred on Britain and the white Dominions; second, the problem of economic and social relations between white settlers and non-Europeans; finally, the economic and moral consequences of economic development in the tropics based on maximum expansion of the commodity trade. In each case he found what might be called a conventional and an alternative tradition. In volume II of the *Survey* he set out to assess the balance of probability in each of them; and I propose next to consider briefly what conclusions he reached and what contribution he made to colonial economic history in the process.

Problems of Economic Policy: The Main Arguments

It is essential if one is to understand Hancock's work to grasp that, at least in the *Survey*, his aims were somewhat different from those of the conventional historian. As he described them in the preface to volume II, the book was to have two characteristics: it was to be normative, in the sense that he hoped to influence practical decisions on future policy, because this was the Chatham House formula for the series; and its fundamental measure of value was to be moral. Was the policy of the British empire, in the words of Sir Eyre Crowe, quoted by Hancock in the introduction, 'so directed as to harmonize with the general desires and ideals common to all mankind . . .'? Ironically this means that the *Survey* has something in common in its approach — though not, I suggest, in its quality as history — with much recent Marxist writing on the historical genesis of 'underdevelopment' and the 'North-South dialogue'. Partly for this reason, but also, I suspect, because his mind preferred to deal in large ideas and abstractions, Hancock began by setting up two sets of concepts which he used throughout the two books as organizing principles. On the more general level he suggested that imperial economic policy could be analysed in terms of Adam Smith's two antithetical poles: 'mercantilism' and 'the great commercial republic'. The first aimed at imperial autarky, mainly in the interests of the parent state; the second treated both metropolis and colonies as part of the international economy, even if they had certain special relationships. The other set of concepts consisted of five variants on Turner's frontier thesis, defining empire and imperialism in terms of different embodiments of European expansion: the settlers' frontier, the frontier of trade, the frontier of investment, the planters' frontier, and the missionary frontier. Although he did not employ these concepts rigorously, most of the material, both on the tropical dependencies, and on South Africa, New Zealand, and Australia, was examined in these terms.

Exposition of these categories took Hancock some ninety-three pages. One might have expected this chapter to end there; but in fact Hancock included a final section on 'The Economics of Siege' in which he traced the evolution of extreme autarkic concepts in Britain during the First World War. These are rightly famous pages, for in them he provided the first critical analysis of how the potentially constructive ideas of Chamberlain and the tariff reformers of the first decade of the century were distorted into the 'ju-ju economics' of the Empire Resources Development Committee. Structurally, however, the significance of dealing with this material at the end of the introductory chapter was that Hancock was then poised to move in two directions; to the Ottawa system and the Dominions, and also to the influence of such ideas on tropical colonies, such as those in West Africa. Indeed, the relatively short second chapter, 'The End of the War', forms a common link between these concepts and post-war developments in each area, describing, first, the failure of attempts to use colonial commodities (palm oil, tin, etc.) as weapons in international political and economic warfare (as suggested by the Empire Resources Development Committee); and, second, the apparent defeat of imperial preference as a link between Britain and the white Dominions by 1924. But from that point the two themes diverge. The remainder of part one is devoted to chapter 3 on 'The Autonomous Nations of the Commonwealth, 1923–1939', leaving the rest of the empire to part two.

This brings us to Hancock's critique of the Ottawa system and its consequences. Characteristically he divided his analysis of the background to Ottawa into three thematic sections, dealing in turn with 'men' (i.e. emigration), 'money' (i.e. investment), and 'markets'. Under each heading he went back into the past to show how belief in the essential complementarity of British and Dominion interests had led to misguided belief that somehow a system could be created which would express and co-ordinate all these needs and how this belief could result, under crisis conditions, in the Ottawa Conference of 1932. In each case he was able to show that attitudes had outlived realities. There was no possibility of genuine complementarity within the white empire, with the result that Ottawa became a disorganized market rather than the occasion for establishing a rational and harmonious imperial system. Section four then demonstrates the consequences of this intellectual confusion during the seven years before 1939. Hancock rejected the facile assumption that the increased proportion of intra-imperial trade was mainly due to the Ottawa preferences and quotas; he showed that the internal contradictions of the system had largely killed belief in it by 1938; and he interpreted the 1938 treaties between Britain and America and America and Canada as evidence of a swing back to international free trade or, in terms of his categories, from mercantilism to the great commercial republic. The chapter ends with an account of measures taken by the Labour government of New Zealand during the later 1930s to offset the catastrophic consequences of the slump in the market for her commodity exports; the point being, I think, that this showed that there were alternatives to the 'siege economics' which were the conceptual basis of imperial autarky.

What, in retrospect, was the importance of this critique of the concept of an imperial economy? Basically that Hancock was the first historian to take a balanced view of the whole issue, taking account of both British and Dominion conditions and seeing recent developments in their long-term historical and conceptual setting. He was helped by the fact that he was writing in and after 1938, for this enabled him to show, *ex post*, how inherently unworkable the Ottawa system was. The impressive thing is that, although he was writing so close to the events and without access to confidential material, his analysis has never been seriously challenged. It stood as the best account until I.M. Drummond published in 1974 his *British Economic Policy and the Empire, 1919–1939*; and even then Drummond did little more than spell out and confirm Hancock's argument. Thus Hancock had punctured the balloon of imperial self-sufficiency; and, although some hot air continued to seep out in the rhetoric of old Commonwealth hands down to the 1970s and the negotiations for Britain's entry to the EEC, the hole was never plugged. This was an impressive historical and intellectual achievement.

In terms of Hancock's organizing principles most of the argument in part one was thus devoted to his antithetical concepts of 'mercantilism' and 'the great commercial republic' and demonstrated his strong preference for the second of these. Part two, by contrast, concentrates on variations on his version of the frontier thesis: chapter 1 deals with the 'Evolution of the Settlers' Frontier: Southern Africa'; chapter 2 with 'Evolution of the Traders' Frontier: West Africa'. Of the two I think it is now clear that the second was more original and has had a far greater subsequent impact. Mainly for this reason I propose to deal briefly with South Africa and concentrate more on West Africa.

In dealing with South Africa Hancock could use a considerable amount of relatively sophisticated published material; and the main value of this chapter is, therefore, that it pulled a great deal of material together, brought it up to date, and put it into a geographical and intellectual framework which included the Rhodesias, Nyasaland, and also, though not in any detail, Kenya. He had already opened up the general theme of relations between white settlers and non-European peoples in part one of volume II: he now concentrated on the two aspects of this problem that seemed most important in South Africa — segregation and the native reserves policy. In each case he underlined the historical roots of contemporary policies; and perhaps the outstanding feature of his account was his determination to be fair to white South Africans. In its modern form segregation and job reservation flowed from the determination of British immigrants to the mines to remain an aristocracy of labour and from the problem of 'poor white' as much as from the conventionally ascribed Afrikaner racialism. These were real problems, which could not be swept under the carpet by liberal prescriptions for racial equality. Similarly the reserves policy could be seen in principle as a legitimate attempt to protect Bantu society against the encroachment of white land-owners: the question was whether the key measure — the Native Trusts and Land Act of 1936 — adequately met the needs of the African majority. Hancock was clear that it did not and that in its present form the reserves policy, along with segregation, could not stand up to the test of public morality. Turning north, he noted that similar policies had been adopted for roughly similar reasons in Southern Rhodesia, despite the formal power of the imperial government to veto such measures. Hancock regretted this; but, in a sentence which had ironical overtones in 1980, remarked that 'In fact it [sc. the UK government] could only make its will effective by resuming direct responsibility for the government of Southern Rhodesia: such a reversal of historical development is inconceivable'.[4] Nyasaland had largely escaped the impact of the settlers' frontier, but in Northern Rhodesia its effects were becoming apparent. The High Commission Territories might escape if, as Margery Perham and others were then demanding, the Dominions Office stood out against Union pressures for incorporation and took positive steps to develop their economies.

In retrospect Hancock's treatment of these policy issues, the last in his book still to be alive, seems reasonable, liberal, but perhaps too neutral: we do not find here the outright condemnation of racialism in all its forms which we would have hoped to see. Nor, it must be said, is there a considered critique of the economic, as contrasted with the social, significance of segregation and its affiliates. The nearest Hancock comes to this is in his conclusion on pages 151-3, when he affirms that the economic unity of all peoples in South Africa overrode other dividing factors. The essential fact was that the future prospects of whites as well as blacks, coloured, and Indians, depended on 'economic co-operation' leading to 'policies which would endeavour to raise the level of the masses and thereby drain the morass which threatens to engulf the less efficient or less fortunate Europeans'. This was the attitude of contemporary foreign capitalists, such as Unilever, whose local market was already seen to depend on black affluence. It was also, I suppose, the underlying belief of Smuts; and it is important to remember that in the later 1930s Smuts was a hero to Hancock, as he was to most British liberals; and that in this era, before the Nationalist victory of 1948, it was still possible to hope for change by evolution in South African racial policies.

There is, I think, a consensus that the most original and influential part of the *Survey* is the second chapter of part two, 'Evolution of the Traders' Frontier: West Africa'. The approach was not, of course, entirely fresh since the concept of the 'legitimate trade' was well established and by 1938, when Hancock started to work on volume II, Lilian Knowles had pointed to some of the potential conflicts of interest that might arise even in an open trading economy where there were few settlers or foreign-owned plantations. Hancock's achievement was that he was able, from the vantage point of the later 1930s and with knowledge of the effects of the slump on commodity producers, to define these problems with much greater precision than anyone had done before. His approach was quickly taken up: for example by J. Mars in *Mining, Commerce and Finance in Nigeria* edited by Margery Perham (1948); and in her preface to the earlier volume *The Native Economies of Nigeria* (1946) she specially emphasized the influence Hancock's work had on West African studies. Thereafter his ideas become part of the common stock of attitudes to West African economic history; and my aim is therefore merely to summarize his argument and to underline what was most novel and influential in it.

Hancock's starting-point was the then common assumption that in West Africa, even if not elsewhere, the British had established economic and social systems which were fully consistent with the concept of trusteeship and avoided the moral and economic disasters of many other colonial systems. He devoted some twenty pages to tracing the evolution of the slave trade into a legitimate trade in commodities. Most writers, including McPhee, took the expansion of this commodity trade as proof that morality had paid off and that the new commercial system was entirely beneficial; and certainly the commercial statistics up to 1929 seemed to demonstrate that what is now called the 'open economy' was an unqualified success. Hancock, however, pointed to three problems which stemmed directly from this achievement: imperfect competition among the big trading firms, which might affect the rewards received by African producers; the effects of the catastrophic drop in the price of commodities after 1930, which called into question the comparative advantage principle and, incidentally, points to the modern concept of 'unequal exchange'; and the growing competition between West African peasant producers and plantations elsewhere, which raised large issues concerning the prospects of the West African economic system and the policies government should adopt. Most of the chapter consists of a detailed analysis of these issues.

But first Hancock went back to the concept of the settlers' frontier and asked whether it was true that the virtual absence of white settlers and land alienation in British West Africa was, as McPhee and others believed, simply the result of British benevolence. By carefully reviewing the historical process he showed that the story was in fact much more complicated. The humanitarian impulse was undoubtedly important; but it was economic factors that made it possible to safeguard African ownership of land. On the Gold Coast the government's policy of vesting all 'waste' land in the Crown had been defeated by the chiefs and alienation of land might well have proceeded indefinitely had it not been for the cocoa boom which, coupled with the official ban on European plantations, stimulated African chiefs to use 'stool' land for cocoa production rather than sell it to Europeans. In Nigeria the government felt able to refuse demands from entrepreneurs such as William Lever to establish plantations because peasant production seemed to provide an economically satisfactory alternative: indeed, to most colonial administrators this seemed a better mode of production, since peasants could adjust their production patterns to variations in the market, whereas a plantation could not. Thus Hancock showed that the 'virtuous' elements in British West African policies were largely contingent on the possibility of a non-settler import-export economy. This, he thought, largely explained the contrast between this and other regions of British Africa.

Turning to the economic consequences of peasant production of a limited range of export commodities, Hancock also found reason to question established certainties. Apart from the terrible drop in prices after 1929, the main question was whether peasants could continue to compete with plantations. Statistics showed that plantation production of palm oil and kernels in South-east Asia had resulted in a very much faster rate of growth and in higher qualities of oil since the First World

War. If this was continued, the West African peasant might eventually be driven from the market. Hancock, incidentally, wrongly thought that the faster growth of palm oil from the Belgian Congo was due to use of plantations there: in fact there were almost no such plantations there by 1939 and the growth of the industry since 1919 was the result rather of intensive exploitation of sylvan palms after a late start. In any case, the success of plantations elsewhere led Hancock to assess the relative merits of peasant and plantation production. He was glad to find that the problem was only acute for palm oil, since peasant production of cocoa, ground nuts, and cotton seemed fully competitive. For palm oil he could see no clear solution, for the undoubted advantages provided by plantations seemed offset by the social benefits of peasant production within a traditional social framework. His best palliative, which he developed later in section 4 of this chapter, was to improve peasant production by scientific methods of cultivation, as was already done for cocoa, and by providing better pressing and kernel-crushing facilities for palm oil: this, he hoped, would provide a viable compromise between tradition and science. But he recognized that this might fail; and he fell back on the perceptive and prophetic thought that, even if West African oil palm products ceased to be competitive on the international market, at least they would provide valuable food for Nigerians. By the 1970s his prediction had proved correct: Nigeria had become a net importer of palm oil.

Hancock then turned to what I think was his most important investigation — the operation of free trade and the 'open economy', though this term came into vogue much later. The problem was to discover whether the commodity trade benefited Africans as much as it was believed to do and as much as it ought to do: that is, whether the facts supported the claim of the classical economists (to whom Hancock constantly recurred) that specialization was the best route to wealth. He recognized that one key to this question lay in the character of the import-export houses who dominated the trade. Why, under free trade, had these firms become so few in number that they could achieve something approaching monopoly as sellers and monopsony as buyers? Hancock approached the first of these questions as an historian rather than the economist he never claimed to be. Concentration was the outcome of cycles of intense competition which drove the weak into bankruptcy and generated amalgamations and rings for, in so volatile and speculative a business, only the strong could survive fluctuations in the market and even they found that unrestricted competition destroyed profits. Thus free trade was the solvent of free

competition: concentration was a law of capitalist economics, a conclusion which (although he did not say so) brought Hancock into line
with such critics of capitalism as J.A. Hobson and the Marxists.

There remained the question of what effects concentration and
cartels had on the African as consumer and producer. Here Hancock
was handicapped, as historians still are, by the absence of detailed
studies of the operations of the large firms such as United Africa
Company (UAC) and John Holt. But Hancock did some research himself and came out with five general conclusions which, even after
Bauer's much more detailed research in the early 1950s,[5] still largely
stand up.

1. Despite concentration, considerable competition still remained, for
   new, smaller, firms were constantly entering the field and could
   compete because of their lower overheads.
2. Trading agreements were defensive, the result of competition so
   intense that without them trading firms would go bankrupt. In any
   case they seldom lasted for long.
3. The African middleman was a major weakness in the system, raising
   prices to buyers and reducing the return to producers. On this,
   incidentally, Bauer was later to disagree.
4. There was some evidence (he quoted figures from Baro) that prices
   paid to producers depended on the number of buyers in any particular place. Conversely the entry of 'Syrian' traders at Kano into
   a preserve of UAC and Holts immediately raised the going price
   for produce. Hancock's discovery, Mr Raccah, the ring-breaking
   Syrian trader at Kano, was to become a famous symbolic figure.
5. Hence the conclusion was that, while concentration and buyers'
   agreements were the condition for the survival of the trading firms,
   they had an adverse effect on the terms of trade (another phrase
   Hancock did not use) of Africans and significantly reduced the
   potential benefits of the open economy.

These were important and highly influential conclusions, though
they could only be tested by far more research and evidence than
Hancock could provide. They left him, given his assumed normative
role, with the obligation to provide solutions or palliatives. Here he
found himself in difficulties, as well he might, since no one has yet
produced an answer which is at once economically viable, socially
acceptable, and fair to the peasant producer. State marketing, the
solution adopted in West Africa in the very year this volume was
published and which Bauer and Helleiner later showed to have disastrous
consequences for peasant producers, lay outside his range of possibilities

in 1939. As in the case of peasant versus plantation, Hancock therefore suggested compromises. Co-operatives might redress the balance between producer and merchant, though their record in the Gold Coast was so far not encouraging. The Nowell Commission of 1938 had suggested a sellers' association which would pool the total crop and so bargain more effectively with the traders, but the individualism of the cocoa farmers had made this impracticable. Minor palliatives might include government inspection of crops to specify different qualities, public regulation of marketing to end abuses practised by middlemen, and a system of licensed buyers who would have to display upset buying prices so that sellers could not be bargained down. Taken collectively these were, in fact, the germs of the system adopted during the Second World War, though in the context of state marketing; and I propose therefore briefly to look ahead to see how Hancock's ideas relate to what actually happened.

The West African Produce Control Board of 1942 fixed all buying prices, licensed all buyers, allocated export quotas to each established firm based on a datum period before 1939, and paid them a commission plus expenses. The commodities were bought by the British Ministry of Food at what were originally regarded as equitable prices to buffer the colonies against the effect of dislocation of the international market, but which soon became unreasonably low, given the inflated price of colonial imports. Thereafter, to look still further ahead, the system evolved after the war into a number of separate marketing boards, one for each major product in each colony; and a stated aim of the system was that the colonial government would build up reserves which could be used to supplement peasants' earnings when market prices were down and so even out fluctuations in the commodity market. We know Hancock's provisional view of this system for he commented on it in his *Wealth of Colonies* in 1950. Bulk purchase by the British ministry was dangerous for Commonwealth relations because it made commercial transactions a political issue. But the system of marketing boards as then defined had a 'definite economic advantage' for the colonies because it offered 'a release from the curse of sudden fluctuations . . .' and

mitigated the evils that arise from too much money chasing too few goods; in the long term they are an investment fund that can be employed in the rehabilitation and expansion of existing industries, or the development of new ones.[6]

There remains one final question: what was the range of Hancock's vision on economic development in tropical Africa, beyond commodity production? How does it relate to later thinking on colonial and post-colonial economic development?

I do not think it unfair to Hancock to suggest that the most striking feature of his prescription for the future is what it omitted, a classic case of the dog that did not bark, or perhaps merely growled quietly: he made little or no reference to the importance or possibility of indus-trialization. In the final pages of his West African chapter (pp. 293-7) he talks, very cautiously, of the important possibilities for Nigeria of the growth of modernized craft industries, such as pottery, and also of small-scale 'modern' enterprises, such as the repair of bicycles. But there is no account of the new modern factory industries already to be found on the West Coast, nor any hint that the economic future of these colonies might lie in industrialization. Even in 1950 he remained sceptical about its possibilities: industrialization was 'not the main front'.[7] For this lack of interest there were, I think, two main reasons. First, there was very little modern factory industry in West Africa in 1940: as Peter Kilby later summed it up, apart from cotton ginneries and sawmills, Nigeria had only

A soap works in Lagos (1924), two palm-oil bulking plants (1924), a cigarette factory at Ibadan (1937) and a metal-drum plant (1939). ... The Gold Coast boasted a Swiss brewery (1932) but lacked production of either soap or cigarettes.[8]

Clearly there was little here to stimulate Hancock's interest or expec-tations.

But there was a second and more important reason. Hancock shared a belief that stemmed from the classical economists and was restated, with modifications, as late as 1949 by (Sir) Arthur Lewis in what was effectively the first modern economic analysis of growth in under-developed countries – *Colonial Development* (1949) which Hancock had read by 1950 – that industry, if it was to be viable and economically beneficial, should grow naturally out of increased efficiency in agricul-ture. Hancock may have been right: certainly the rhapsodic enthusiasm of the 1950s and 1960s for industrialization at all costs has now been effectively deflated by evidence of its high economic costs and no longer features so large even in the work of contemporary underdevelop-ment theorists. Still, it remains a significant gap in Hancock's analysis that he did not rigorously work out the arguments for and against industrialization in the colonies, the more surprising in that he was well aware of the record of industry fostered by protectionism in Australia. I can only note the fact, not explain it.

Thus Hancock's general conclusion and prescription for future economic policy in tropical dependencies was that Britain must ensure that imperial interests did not result in harm to colonial subjects: empire must not mean exploitation. This was vital but, as he realized, also negative. More was needed to fulfil the imperial trust and to overcome poverty in the colonies. Free trade was no longer sufficient, given the collapse of the commodity market. The colonial state must therefore pursue active policies. It must educate, improve health, expand transport, survey land, promote better methods of agriculture, umpire the process of marketing. All these implied something more than *laissez-faire*. Yet even this was not enough. The real solution to colonial poverty required international action; and the *Survey* ends with proposals for international co-operation after the war to improve living standards everywhere.

The *Survey* and its Successors

In conclusion, how does the *Survey* stand after forty years? Should it now be seen as a major historiographical turning-point? How great an advance did it make on its predecessors and what influence did it have on its successors?

Although it is now difficult for anyone who was, so to speak, brought up on Hancock to imagine a literature on colonial history which does not include the *Survey*, one has only to do so to see its importance. Behind Hancock lay perhaps four traditions of imperial history: the constitutional tradition, exemplified by A.B. Keith, and taken to its highest intellectual level by Kenneth Wheare in his *The Statute of Westminster and Dominion Status* (1938-1953 edns); the tradition of enthusiasm for the empire-Commonwealth, embodied in the writings of Lionel Curtis or L.S. Amery and, in a different form, in the then still emerging *CHBE*, of which the Dominion and Indian volumes, together with volume I on the empire before 1783, were already published; what I might call the tradition of historical geography, which, like Sarraut's *La Mise en valeur des colonies françaises* (1923), tended to concentrate on the economic potential of the colonies from a metropolitan standpoint, as did Knowles and McPhee; and finally the 'trusteeship' literature, of which Lugard's *The Dual Mandate* (1922) was to become the eventual symbol, though it is interesting that Hancock never mentions this book, while referring to the *Political Memoranda* of 1918.

Seen against this background Hancock's book stands out as the first major work of synthesis which took account of all these traditions and brought into a single historical and conceptual framework the whole gamut of British colonizing experience from the seventeenth century to the eve of the Second World War. At the same time he deflated many pretentious ideas and exaggerated claims by taking an essentially secular, not sacerdotal, view of imperial issues, and this despite his concentration on moral issues. Despite the attempt by some later practitioners to revive the older theological tradition, imperial history was never the same again.

But what of economic history, which is my main concern? Here one must be more cautious. Hancock had no economic training (which he was the first to admit). There was no established study of the economics of development by the 1930s and the very concept of 'growth' as it is now understood was in its infancy. Even S.H. Frankel's seminal *Capital Investment in Africa* (1938) (itself a by-product of Hailey's *An African Survey* (1938), so from the same stable as Hancock's work), seems by later standards to lack a central organizing principle. An additional handicap was the very limited body of statistical information then available on colonial economies. It must be said, also, that Hancock did not make full use of ideas and information already available. India might have provided him with valuable insights into the economic and political problems resulting from a colonial economy, and plenty had been written on these by the 1930s. He never refers to them. Nor does he investigate the economic and ethical problems associated with imperial control of a colony's money supply, though he indicates in *Wealth of Colonies* that by 1950 he had become aware of their significance. Finally he was, of course, unable to use unpublished official records, since these were then open only to the 1880s. In short, it would be unrealistic to expect Hancock to have written the sort of economic history which we would look for from a contemporary economic historian, trained in economics and with a wealth of tools and information which he did not have at his disposal. What, then, was his achievement and what influence does he seem to have had on the work of later economic historians?

I think the *Survey* made two important contributions to the economic history of the modern British colonies. First, as I have suggested, it provided the first balanced historical account of the genesis

and working of the Ottawa system. Second, the chapter on West Africa
was a real triumph. It was limited by lack of emphasis on the African as
a consumer, on traditional segments of the economy, on industrialization, monetary policy, the terms of trade, and many other things.
But his account and critique of the structure of the export trade was
a real *tour de force*, opening up new vistas and destroying old certainties.
This, I suspect, was the most influential thing Hancock wrote on
colonial economics. Apart from the two books on the Nigerian economy
edited by Margery Perham in the later 1940s, which were never very
widely used, Hancock's *Survey* stood for at least two decades as the
main source for modern West African economic history. Here at least
one is justified in using the word 'seminal'. By contrast, I think the
South African section has had much less impact, partly because what
he wrote was less original than other parts of the study, but also
because it was less about economics than morals.

How far has the later writing of colonial economic history followed
Hancock's model? I have suggested that two main limitations in his
work were, first, lack of sophisticated economic concepts, second,
shortage of statistics. As to the first, he said at the start of his lectures
on the *Wealth of Colonies* 'You are economists, I am an historian.'[9]
The modern economic historian is better equipped and he can now
choose from a wide range of theories on how an underdeveloped
economy may be induced to grow. This gives him a different perspective: it will certainly enable him to sound more sophisticated. He
is likely to start from the assumption that the central issue is growth
and he will tend to analyse imperial economic policies from the standpoint of whether or not they contributed to growth. Hancock did not
deal in growth and this cuts him off from most modern exponents
of the art.

The second obvious difference stems from the volume of detailed
information that has been built up since the 1930s. In my opinion
'Third World' statistics are spectacularly unreliable, even by the general
standard of statistics: recently the whole statistical basis of G. Blyn's
previously 'authoritative' *Agricultural Trends in India, 1891-1947*
(1966) has been challenged.[10] Yet, as the bibliography of A.G. Hopkins's
An Economic History of West Africa (1973) — itself a worthy descen-
dant of Hancock's *Survey* — suggests, there is now a considerable
volume of carefully researched information on West African economic
and social history which was simply not available in the 1930s. Such
research has radically changed preoccupations and attitudes, reducing
the innovative role of the European and explaining many features of

West African life which were necessarily enigmatic to Hancock. The measure of the difference is clear from comparing Hopkins's book with Hancock's West African chapter; and I am certain Hancock would be the first to agree that Hopkins was able to improve on his account if only because he could draw on much more detailed and reliable sources.

Modern 'Third World' economic history is, therefore, more economic, more conceptual, and has a better factual basis than it had in the 1930s and in Hancock's work. But perhaps the most significant change results from the mere passage of time and altered perspectives. Hancock, as I have emphasized, felt that he had a normative role: he had to analyse in order to offer prescriptions to deal with urgent problems of empire. In the post-colonial era the economic historian is relieved of this obligation: only those who, like A.G. Frank, have adopted what one might call a neo-theological posture, still use colonial history for normative functions. Others can take an entirely secular approach: the contemporary economic historian is freed from the incubus of public policy. This should enable him to write more detached and professional history than Hancock: he will certainly have to write it more briefly because few publishers would now accept a manuscript as extended and discursive as Hancock's *Survey*. Yet smaller is not necessarily more beautiful. I very much doubt whether anything published recently on colonial economic history will have as much influence in the future, or be thought as important in forty years' time, as Hancock's *Survey* is now.

Notes

1. Deborah Lavin has shown in her essay (p. 117 above) that Curtis had suggested that Chatham House should publish a *Survey of British Commonwealth Affairs* and that Hancock should be invited to write the first volume. Curtis had entertained Hancock when he was a Rhodes Scholar in 1923 and regarded him as a convert to Round Table principles. At the start, in 1934, this was probably true. But by the later 1930s Hancock seems largely to have thrown off this influence; and Lavin quotes him (p. 118 above) as saying that he then regarded himself as 'at war with Curtis and Co. not only on issues of constitution-making and foreign policy but on the racial issue'.

2. W.K. Hancock, *Country and Calling* (London, 1954), pp. 150–1.

3. In the preface to volume II of the *Survey*, Hancock wrote that 'The Indian chapter, though it would carry further a study of the Indian national question contained in volume I, will probably not be written. It is to be hoped that some other writer, equipped with a first-hand and sympathetic knowledge of Indian national, religious, economic and governmental problems, will undertake

in one sustained effort, a *Survey of Indian Affairs 1918-1931.*' The hope was not fulfilled.

4. Hancock, *Survey*, II (1), p. 98.

5. See his *West African Trade* (Cambridge, 1954).

6. W.K. Hancock, *Wealth of Colonies* (Cambridge, 1950), pp. 55-6.

7. Ibid., p. 69.

8. P. Kilby in Peter Duignan and L.H. Gann (eds.), *Colonialism in Africa* (Cambridge, 1971), IV, p. 49.

9. In a lecture given in 1952 to the American Historical Association Hancock made the following statement.

> I may as well confess — since this is a moment of professional self-examination — that my own West African studies were deficient in theoretical sophistication. I could have made them more interesting to economists if I had provided myself in advance with their favourite boxes into which to put the economic data that I was collecting. Instead, either I made boxes of my own (sometimes I felt myself compelled to do this, because many of the facts had such queer and unexpected shapes) or else I used the old fashioned boxes of classical economics. I shall argue later on that some of these boxes have proved very durable and that economists in recent decades have discarded them rather too hastily. Nevertheless, it would have been at least of technical advantage to me to show myself more fluent in the economic language of the nineteen-thirties.

'Agenda for the Study of British Imperial Economy 1850-1950', *Journal of Economic History*, XIII (1953), 1, p. 263.

10. Clive Dewey, 'Patwari and Chaukidar', in C. Dewey and A.G. Hopkins (eds.), *The Imperial Impact* (London, 1978), pp. 280-314.

NOTES ON CONTRIBUTORS

GREIG BARR succeeded Sir Kenneth Wheare as Rector of Exeter College in 1972. When at Magdalen College as an undergraduate reading Modern History, he won the Stanhope Prize in 1938 and took a First the following year. In 1946, after service with the Royal Devon Yeomanry, he was elected to a fellowship at Exeter College and has lectured and taught there for over a quarter of a century, particularly in English constitutional history of the Tudor and Stuart periods. From 1948 to 1972 he was treasurer of the Oxford University Rugby Football Club. He served with Sir Edgar Williams for some sixteen years as a Curator of the University Chest and for five years as a member of Hebdomadal Council. Since 1975 he has also been a Rhodes Trustee.

DAVID FIELDHOUSE, now Vere Harmsworth Professor of Imperial and Naval History and Fellow of Jesus College in Cambridge, has spent most of his life either at Oxford or in an overseas Commonwealth country. Born in India of missionary parents, he was repatriated in 1929. His undergraduate years at The Queen's College, Oxford, sandwiched three years as a Royal Naval pilot, some of it spent in Canada and the United States. After a couple of years teaching history at Haileybury, living among the shades of the Indian administrators trained there in its East India College days, he spent five years as a lecturer at the University of Canterbury, New Zealand. While there he was transformed into an imperial historian, but with a markedly peripheral view of empire. He returned to Oxford in 1958 to become Beit Lecturer in Commonwealth History. Apart from sabbatical visits to Canberra (1965), Yale (1969/70), and Stanford (1976/7) he stayed there until 1981 and for the last fifteen years was a Fellow of Nuffield College. His early publications were on New Zealand and the Pacific; but from 1961 he was persuaded to write on larger themes in the general field of imperialism. He has written a comparative history of modern European (and American) empires, collected illustrative extracts on theories of capitalist imperialism, and assessed their relative validity in various regions of the world in Africa, Asia, and the Pacific. He wrote a history of Unilever overseas, for which he won the John Wadsworth Prize awarded by the Business Archives Council in 1980. With Frederick Madden he was historical consultant for the Time-Life series on the British Empire. They found their advice rarely heeded but attempted jointly in the final number an imperial balance sheet, which they found reflected a remarkably felicitous identity of views. He is at present committed to writing books on the economics of modern colonialism and on decolonization and its consequences.

ANTHONY KIRK-GREENE, Senior Research Fellow at St Antony's College since 1964, spent three years in the Indian army before going up to Cambridge where he learnt something about the theory of indirect rule from Jack Gallagher and Ronald Robinson's lectures before going out to practise it as a District Officer in Nigeria. His election to a Commonwealth fellowship in 1958 enabled him to spend a year in the United States. Returning to Africa he was first Supervisor to the new training course for Nigerian administrative officers and then Reader in Government at Ahmadu Bello University. On leaves he participated frequently in Robinson's Cambridge Summer Schools on African administration and was involved from its beginnings in the Oxford Colonial Records Project. He joined the Commonwealth history team at Oxford during Gallagher's tenure of the chair and now teaches for the new paper on Imperialism and Nationalism. In 1972 he spent six months in East and Central Africa as consultant to the East African Community. He has lectured extensively in North America and was in 1977 the inaugural Killam Visiting Fellow at Calgary University. He has written widely on Nigerian history, on the Sudan Political Service, on the transfer of power in Africa, on the martial races and the military in the empire, and on British colonial governors in Africa as well as on Canada's Governors-General. He is currently working on a history of the Colonial Service and is director of the new Development Records Project at the Institute of Commonwealth Studies.

DEBORAH LAVIN, Principal of Trevelyan College, Durham, since 1980 and Senior Associate of St Antony's College, Oxford, was born in South Africa and was educated at Rodean School, Johannesburg, at Rhodes University, Grahamstown, and at Lady Margaret Hall, Oxford (1959-62). She was a lecturer in history at the University of Witwatersrand and then at The Queen's University, Belfast. At Durham she lectures on the history of the empire and Commonwealth and on sub-Saharan and Southern Africa. She has written on the South African war, on the career of Sir Percy FitzPatrick, and on contemporary problems in South Africa and Ireland. She has recently completed a life of Lionel Curtis and is at present editing a book arising out of the papers given at the recent Sudan Historical Records Conference held at Durham where Old Sudanese hands (both Sudanese and British) discussed key themes in the history of the Condominium and the transfer of power.

FREDERICK MADDEN, Professorial Fellow of Nuffield College and Reader in Commonwealth Government since 1957, won the Boulter and Gladstone Prizes (1937, 1938) and the Beit Senior Scholarship (1939) when he was at Christ Church. From 1946 to 1948 he was assistant librarian at Rhodes House and from 1947 to 1957 was Beit Lecturer teaching in the Hawkesley Room there. Since 1950 he had been Academic Adviser to the Devonshire Courses and their several successors (including currently that for Hong Kong), and was Director of the Institute of Commonwealth Studies from 1962 to 1969. He has lectured 'from sea to sea' in Canada and variously in Australia and South Africa, in Rhodesia and Jamaica and at Harvard, Duke and Williamsburg, and has chaired informal conferences of Commonwealth representatives in Denmark. He wrote his B. Litt. thesis (1939) on early New Zealand, and his doctorate (1950) on the Evangelicals and imperial problems in the first half of the nineteenth century. He collaborated with Harlow in publishing documents on British Colonial Developments 1774-1834; and edited (and wrote the concluding chapter to) Harlow's posthumous second volume on the founding of the Second British Empire. He has written on medieval and Tudor empire, on the American colonies, on the imperial machinery of the Younger Pitt, on the period from 1895 to 1914 for the *Cambridge History of the British Empire*, and most recently on the non-exportability of the Westminster model and the 'patriation' of the BNA Act. At the request of the Modern

History Board he published a small volume of imperial constitutional documents and for the past twenty-five years has been writing an imperial constitutional history from the late twelfth to the mid-twentieth centuries and collecting and (with David Fieldhouse) editing documents to illustrate his themes. After a prolonged search for a publisher, it is now hoped to start publication of these volumes in the near future if sufficient financial support can be found.

COLIN NEWBURY, Senior Lecturer in Commonwealth History and Fellow of Linacre College, was born in New Zealand, took his first degrees at the University of Otago as a student of Professor W.P. Morrell, *quondam* Beit Lecturer, and completed his doctorate at the Australian National University, Canberra, after a year in French archives and field research in Eastern Polynesia. He has held teaching posts at Otago and in the Universities of Ibadan and Hawaii and at the Center for Commonwealth Studies, Duke University. In 1959 he was employed by UNESCO to survey the teaching of the social sciences in African universities before coming to Oxford to write up his research material on West African history. He was elected to the Senior Research Officership at the Institute of Commonwealth Studies in 1965, was an Academic Adviser to the courses on Government and Development there in 1969, and succeeded to the lecturership on George Bennett's death in 1970. His teaching and research interests include the economic history of African and Commonwealth states, the study of international migration and settlement, comparative political and social change in the Pacific, the sterling crises of the post-Second World War period and decolonization, and foreign jurisdiction. He has published books (and collected documents) on the economic, constitutional, and administrative history of West Africa, on Pacific missions, and on French Polynesia. He is at present completing histories of labour, plantations, and mining in New Guinea and of diamond mining in South Africa.

RONALD ROBINSON, Beit Professor of Commonwealth History and Fellow of Balliol College in Oxford since 1971, was formerly scholar and Fellow of St John's Cambridge (1949-71), Lecturer in the Expansion of Europe (1953-69), and Smuts Reader in Commonwealth Studies there (1966-71). After war service with bomber command (which was preceded by training in Rhodesia and South Africa) and bureaucratic experience in the Colonial Office African division (1947-9), he wrote his doctoral thesis on British trusteeship in East and Central Africa 1889-1939. He was a member of the Bridges Committee on Training in Public Administration in 1961, and chaired, and edited the reports of, the annual Cambridge Conferences on Developing Countries from 1961 to 1970. More recently he has re-established in 1978 the Oxford Colonial Development Records Project, a revival of the earlier Colonial Records Project for the rescue of papers of colonial administrators; an enterprise for which Dame Margery Perham and Frederick Madden had been initially responsible. He has written variously on British imperialism of the nineteenth and twentieth centuries especially in Africa, often with his friend the late Professor Gallagher. Their joint works include the seminal article in the *Economic History Review* (1953) on the imperialism of free trade, a contribution to the *New Cambridge Modern History* (1962) on the partition of Africa; and *Africa and the Victorians* (1961). He has further developed and demonstrated the implications of these studies, particularly in the concept of 'collaboration' and the non-European foundations of European empire, and has written a number of articles on the rise and fall of African colonial empire and the transfer of power, particularly in preparation for a biography of Sir Andrew Cohen with whom he worked as Research Officer in the Colonial Office. He and Frederick Madden contributed chapters on general imperial issues in consecutive periods covering the years 1880-1914 in the *Cambridge History of the British Empire* (Vol. III). With Sir Edgar Williams he served as an observer at the Rhodesian elections in 1980.

RICHARD SYMONDS, Honorary Senior Research Officer at the Oxford University Institute of Commonwealth Studies since 1979 and a Senior Associate of St Antony's College, was born in Oxford and read Modern History at Corpus Christi College. He served in India during the Bengal Famine with the Friends' Ambulance Unit and then with the Government of Bengal. He worked again with the Friends in 1947-8 in the movement of minorities between India and Pakistan and then with the United Nations Development Programme in a number of developing countries including East and Southern Africa, Sri Lanka, Yugoslavia, Greece, and Tunis. He interrupted this service with a period as Senior Research Officer at the ICS Oxford and as Professorial Fellow at the Institute for Development Studies, Sussex. He has written on the origins of Pakistan, on the relations of the British and their successors in the Empire, and on the United Nations and the population question. He is now working on a book about Oxford and the empire.